Symphonic Paradox

The Misadventures of a Wayward Musician

By

Sam Denov

ISBN: 0-7596-7543-0

This book is printed on acid free paper.

1stBooks - rev. 11/28/01

Dedication

This book is dedicated to all those individuals who cannot tolerate injustice in the workplace and who work diligently to see that justice is done. Know that you are not alone.

I especially want to thank my wife of nearly six decades, Charlotte, for cutting me the slack I needed while writing this book. I also want to thank my two sons, Tyrone and Ernie, for their suggestions and feedback.

I have been thinking about writing this book for many years, but I finally devoted myself to this project at the urging of two good friends who also happen to be musicians, Libby Blatt and Bruce Steeg.

S.D.

Table of Contents

Chapter 1

The Hiring

It happened early one morning in the late summer of 1954. Walter Hancock, the Personnel Manager of the Chicago Symphony Orchestra, phoned to ask me whether I would be interested in joining the Orchestra's percussion section. I was absolutely nonplused. Before I even had time to consider his offer, I gathered my composure and replied, "Yes. I would." After all, how often does one receive a proposition like that?

Hancock, it seemed, always phoned either very early in the morning before one had their wits together, or late at night when one's head was full of cobwebs. I had been playing with the Orchestra as an extra for the preceding two seasons, including several recordings, mainly because the Principal of the CSO's percussion section was a old and good friend who had recommended me to Hancock. Harry Brabec and I were friends since high school days in Chicago. He was a student at suburban Morton High School while I went to the Lane Technical High School in Chicago. But, we both studied with the same percussion instructor during high school, the one who taught Benny Goodman's famous drummer, Gene Krupa. Roy C. Knapp, our percussion instructor, became famous himself as a result.

Prior to my return to Chicago two years earlier, I spent three seasons with the San Antonio Symphony and two seasons with the Pittsburgh Symphony after my discharge from the U.S. Navy after World War II ended. Having enlisted soon after the war began, I attended the Navy School of Music in Washington, D.C. before being assigned to the Band of the Commander, Fourth Fleet after my graduation.

When I had time to reflect on my decision to join the Chicago Symphony, I thought about the two Percussionists who had recently been fired by the CSO's new Conductor and Music Director, Dr. Fritz Reiner, after just one season. It seemed that Percussionists were not enjoying a very secure career in this Orchestra. Was I going to be the next victim for the chopping block? Of course, had these openings never occurred, I might never have become a member of the Chicago Symphony.

Joining me during my first season in the CSO was James J. Ross, a veteran percussionist who had originally been hired by Reiner in 1927 for the Cincinnati Symphony, the orchestra that Reiner conducted then. Years later, Reiner brought Ross to the Pittsburgh Symphony. Now, Ross was hired again to shore up the CSO's Percussion section, which Reiner found wanting. Although Ross and I worked together in the Pittsburgh Symphony, it seemed like a very precarious situation that I was about to find myself in.

I had no idea how long I would remain with this orchestra, but I was determined to give it my best effort. After dreaming of playing in this orchestra since I first started to study music, my first assignment was to play the brilliant cymbal part in the Second Orchestral Fragments of Maurice Ravel's *Dáphnis and Clóe*. This was Reiner's first week of concerts in his second year with the CSO. I thought that surely, the first week's rehearsals would be a "make or break" situation for me. Of course, since I wasn't hired directly by Reiner, I joined the orchestra solely on Brabec's recommendation. So my first week, in effect, was my audition. If I couldn't convince Reiner that I was the one who could fill this slot in the Percussion section, I would probably never finish this season, much less make it into the next season with this orchestra.

A pianist who needed to play an orchestral instrument in order to enroll in the Lizst Academy in his native Budapest as a youth, Reiner played Timpani and Percussion during those school years. He had a reputation of being extremely hard on percussionists. In was in that crucible that I began my career as a member of the Chicago Symphony Orchestra.

In those years, an orchestra's Music Director was endowed with the sole power to hire and fire musicians without recourse. If one didn't make the grade in the opinion of the Music Director, the hapless musician was simply tendered a notice of non-renewal. A musician was considered hired on a one-year personal service contract, which if not renewed for the succeeding season, was deemed to be a discharge.

Needless to say, every musician knew exactly whom he had to please to remain a member of the orchestra. The symphony orchestra of those days following World War II was not a democratic workplace in which employees were allowed to express any opinion, and especially one contrary to that of the Music Director. He served as the unchallenged dictatorial head of this group of more than a hundred talented musicians. If you challenged the Music Director or did anything at all that displeased him, he had the unbridled power to end your career with that orchestra.

If you felt secure enough to ask for a raise in your weekly salary for the next season, it was with the Music Director that you discussed such matters. On rare occasions, a Music Director may have initiated a raise for a particular musician without ever having been asked. More often than not, it was the Music Director's cronies in the orchestra that received an occasional raise in salary.

My early days in the Chicago Symphony Orchestra were full of fear and trepidation because of Fritz Reiner. I soon learned that I was not alone. Considering that my weekly salary during the first season was $145 for the

2

twenty-eight week winter season, I often thought that the job I now had, although it had been a life-time career goal, might not have been worth it.

Reiner had a penchant for constantly testing the musicians in his charge. More than anything, he demanded an orchestra of musicians who were not only excellent, but also dependable. If he sensed that a musician was in fear of him, and therefor not able to function well under all circumstances, he would relentlessly pick on that musician to see if he could break him. Of course, if that musician did actually break down as a result and was unable to perform at his usual level, he could find himself with a notice of non-renewal at the end of the season.

At other times, it seemed that Reiner would descend on any musician without warning, just to have some personal demonic fun, and in the process, keep all the others on their toes. One never knew when it was going to be his "turn in the barrel" as it came to be called, because it was like being a duck that was in a barrel; an easy target, so to speak.

There was a perverted rationale to Reiner's behavior. It kept everyone on the edge of their seats, completely focused on what the Music Director was doing at every moment. One never knew when they could be singled out. When Reiner decided to descend on a particular musician, and it could be anyone at all, the rest of the orchestra had no choice but to witness the proceeding.

As a typical example, Reiner decided to test the orchestra's new Principal Oboe, Ray Still, during his first season after being promoted to that position in 1954. He had joined the orchestra as Assistant Principal a year earlier after having played in the Baltimore Symphony.

The orchestra was rehearsing the Beethoven *Pastoral* Symphony No. 6 that morning. There is a charming solo for the Oboe, which was beautifully executed by Still. Nonetheless, Reiner shook his head and rapped his baton on his music stand to stop the orchestra. However, he didn't say what it was that had displeased him. He wanted to repeat that passage with the Oboe solo.

Again, Still performed the solo beautifully. And again, Reiner stopped the orchestra, shaking his head. He looked over the ever-present half moon glasses perched on his nose directly at Still and asked, "Haven't you ever played this piece before, Mr. Still?"

Now it turned out that Ray Still is an individual with a good-sized ego who was not easily cowed, even by the likes of someone as important as Reiner. Of course, Reiner did not yet know that. Still looked directly at Reiner and replied, "Of course I have, Dr. Reiner. After all, I played in Baltimore!"

Never one at a loss for words, Reined retorted, "Yes; with the Orioles no doubt!" With that, the orchestra burst into laughter, and the incident was over. Ray Still had passed his test and did not wither under Reiner's gaze. Reiner always respected those who stood their ground against him. They were the types of musicians Reiner wanted in his orchestra. Reiner never picked on Ray Still again for the rest of his days in Chicago. He knew he had someone he could count on.

Reiner was a short, stocky man with virtually no neck who liked to wear a particular style of custom made, black silk rehearsal jacket known as a Nehru jacket. He would sit on a high stool with a backrest and a footrack during rehearsals. He also favored bow ties, which usually hung loose, untied. He very rarely smiled and often looked agitated. Orchestra members believed that if Reiner should ever smile that perhaps his face might crack!

While very few musicians actually liked Reiner personally, most of them had the utmost respect for him musically. He was a thoroughly trained giant of a musician who was capable of directing a wide variety of repertoire unequaled by any other conductor of his day. He was not capable of being jealous of other conductors because he knew very well that he had few if any peers. As a consequence, and because he was so secure, he regularly invited all the greatest conductors of the day to guest conduct the Chicago Symphony in his absence. These guest conductors gave the CSO the flexibility it now has as an ensemble.

Like many before me, I also had my "turn in the barrel" unexpectedly one morning. I had already survived my earliest seasons under Reiner without any problems, so my turn came now as a complete surprise! We were rehearsing Richard Strauss's *The Aristocratic Gentleman*, which was scored for a relatively small ensemble. Playing a pair of hand cymbals in such a small ensemble was something like walking on eggs. If one was too heavy, the eggs may very well crack and ruin everything.

One of the movements required me to play a soft, *pianissimo* note on the first beat of every measure with a pair of cymbals. I was doing my best to play each note very softly when I noticed that Reiner was carefully scrutinizing my playing. It was not long before he stopped the orchestra and gave me very specific instructions on what he wanted me to do.

I thought I was successfully carrying out his instructions when he again stopped the orchestra. This time, instead of giving me further instructions, he asked, "Why do you tilt your cymbals to the right when you play, instead of to your left?"

I quickly realized that it was now my turn for Reiner to have some sadistic pleasure with. It was also a test. I responded by squarely looking back at his eyes and quietly saying, "Because that's the way I play cymbals, Dr. Reiner!" He looked at me with a quizzical look, shrugged his shoulders and continued on with the rehearsal. That was the first and last time he ever challenged me.

It seemed that a number of Reiner incidents revolved around compositions by Richard Strauss. In 1958, while he was preparing the orchestra for an important domestic tour that was to include Boston's Symphony Hall, New York's

Carnegie Hall and the Philadelphia Academy of Music, he programmed Strauss's *Ein Heldenleben*. There is a section in that piece that requires the Trumpet section to play off-stage, simulating a distant fanfare. After experimenting with several different off-stage locations, the Trumpet section and Reiner agreed that the ideal location, at least in Chicago's Orchestra Hall, was Reiner's own small personal dressing room directly behind the stage.

As that particular section came up at a rehearsal, the Trumpet section quietly departed the stage and headed for Reiner's room in preparation for their fanfare. Right after they left the stage, Reiner suddenly realized that he had to use the bathroom. He quickly called for an intermission and headed straight back to his dressing room. As he came to the door, he realized that the three Trumpet players were still there in his room.

As Reiner quickly waved the musicians out of his room, Bud Herseth, the star Principal Trumpet said, "Of course, Dr. Reiner. We'll be happy to evacuate for you."

"Oh no. Only I can do that!" was the response. As soon as the trumpet players left and the door to Reiner's room was securely shut, they completely broke up with laughter.

Reiner was always able to respond to any situation because of his enormous intellect and limitless memory. On very rare occasions, however, he could be fooled. He had an almost infallible ability to recall just about everything he had ever been exposed to. To attempt to put one over on this man was to risk your career. But my friend and section leader, Harry Brabec, actually tried it and for a time, got away with it.

Every Wednesday evening during the winter season, there was a television show that was broadcast by the Chicago Tribune's TV outlet, WGN, Channel 9. It was called *Great Music from Chicago* and was syndicated throughout the nation. It featured a reduced Chicago Symphony Orchestra with Reiner or other Guest Conductors. These shows required the CSO musicians who actually played the show to travel up Michigan Avenue from Orchestra Hall to the WGN studios. The larger instruments were transported by truck, including a trunk full of the percussion equipment needed for the particular show.

On this occasion, the program included Tschaikovsky's *Nutcracker Suite*. A single player, for the most part, could perform all the percussion parts. The rehearsal, which was scheduled immediately before the broadcast, started with the Suite's *Overture Miniature*. The only percussion part called for a Triangle.

As soon as Brabec started to play the Triangle part, Reiner stopped the music and inquired, "Where did you get that garden variety Triangle? Don't you have something bigger?"

The con began when Brabec answered, "Of course, Dr. Reiner!" He then called offstage to me to go to the trunk and get the larger Triangle. That order to me was just loud enough for Reiner to hear it. I immediately went to the hallway outside of the studio and rummaged through the trunk looking for a larger Triangle. I panicked when I couldn't find one.

I called in to Brabec from just offstage and reported in a stage whisper that I couldn't find a larger Triangle. He nodded to me and whispered "I know!" I couldn't imagine what was going to happen next.

The next passage in the music that called for the Triangle found Brabec holding up the same instrument he had used before. The difference this time was that he held it up very high so Reiner could clearly see it, as if to say that *'Here is the Triangle you wanted.'* Reiner looked at Brabec and threw him a salute for having complied with his request. And it worked. A salute from Reiner was about as good a compliment as any musician ever received.

Reiner also seemed to possess knowledge that most other mere mortals were not aware of. There was another incident concerning a Triangle that proved the point. At a rehearsal one morning, Reiner again started complaining about the sound of Brabec's Triangle. Now Reiner asked Brabec to have his Triangle silver plated because he didn't like the sound of the one he was hearing.

Brabec recoiled from that request because he believed that silver plating his Triangle would ruin the sound of it forever. After all, a Triangle is simply a rod of tempered steel alloy that is heated and bent into its triangular shape. Additional heating, however, could change the tempering, and thus the sound, forever. This presented a dilemma for Brabec. How could he comply with Reiner's request without ruining his favorite Triangle forever?

Brabec finessed the situation. After the rehearsal, he walked over to Wabash Avenue and up to Frank's Drum Shop. He told the proprietor that he wanted a Triangle silver-plated, a strange request indeed. "Have you got the Triangle with you?" he was asked.

"Well, no, not yet!" Brabec replied. At that point, Brabec walked into the shop's storeroom where all manner of percussion hardware was kept. He located the bin where 10" Triangles were kept, put his hand into the bin with his eyes closed and picked up one of the Triangles. He gave his choice to the proprietor, saying, "This is the one." He wanted to comply with the Maestro's request without ruining his own instrument. Once this randomly chosen Triangle was silver-plated, he thought he would be able to tell Reiner that silver plating the Triangle simply wouldn't work. But, it didn't turn out quite the way that Brabec had imagined it would.

It was several weeks later that Brabec received a phone message from Frank's Drum Shop saying that the Triangle was now ready, completely silver-plated. Brabec rubbed his hands with glee. He was about to pull a fast one on the Old Man. He walked over to the shop to pick up his package, all neatly wrapped for delivery. Every moment of the trip back to Orchestra Hall was one of gleeful anticipation of the wonderful joke that was about to be played on Reiner.

Upon arrival at Orchestra Hall, Brabec immediately headed to the basement Percussion Room where his colleagues were waiting to hear the results of *Reiner's Folly* as it was being called. Brabec finally ripped off the paper wrapping and there it was! We had never seen such a gleaming Triangle before. But, "How awful did it sound?" That was the question.

To everyone's amazement, this silver plated Triangle had the most gorgeous sound any of us had ever heard. Brabec's stunt had backfired on him, to his chagrin. In the end, somehow, Reiner had been right! How could he have ever known? No one had ever heard a silver plated Triangle before. That Triangle is still being used today by the members of the CSO's Percussion section.

Brabec continued to have his problems with Reiner. He was the lone survivor of the pre-Reiner Kubelik era in the orchestra's Percussion section. From time to time, Reiner began picking on Brabec for what most would consider insignificant problems. Brabec got a strong hint that his days were numbered when on one occasion, he came into Reiner's backstage dressing room with an unloaded shotgun slung over his arm.

As Brabec entered, he asked, "Dr. Reiner, would you like us to use these shotguns for the cannon shots in the 1812 Overture?" That had been the traditional method in Chicago of simulating the cannon shots required by Tschaikovsky's score. Blank cartridges were fired backstage into an empty large steel oil drum.

Reiner, who was sitting in an overstuffed armchair, looked up at Brabec and the gun over his half moon glasses, and replied, "No. I don't think so. The Overture is noisy enough without the guns. Besides, I don't trust you!" Brabec was stunned by that remark for it seemed that the handwriting was already on the wall. It was not long afterward that Brabec received his notice of non-renewal. He lasted only three years under Reiner. Now, there was no one remaining of the original percussion players. After holding auditions in New York, a Juilliard graduate by the name of Gilbert Breines was chosen to replace Brabec as the Principal Percussionist. His tenure also turned out to be short lived.

It was Reiner's cavalier methods of hiring and firing musicians, among other matters, that led up to the problems that surfaced a few years later and forever changed the profession of symphonic musicians in America.

Chapter 2

Reiner Antics

After Brabec's departure, things were never quite the same as they were. Although Breines and I became good friends as well as colleagues, he did not turn out to be the kind of section leader that Brabec had been. However, Reiner made an excellent choice as far as hiring someone whom was highly skilled and thoroughly schooled. But Breines was very young and as it turned out, subject to the military draft. Although the nation was officially at peace, between the Korean conflict and that in Viet Nam, young men like Breines were being conscripted into military service to bolster our nation's defense.

Toward the end of his first season, Breines received his draft notice and was prepared to enter the U.S. Army for a two-year hitch. When Reiner heard that Breines was going into the Army, he was very displeased, to put it mildly. He told Breines that he couldn't go into the Army now because he was planning to perform several compositions next season that had important percussion parts, and he needed him.

Breines tried to explain his predicament as best he could. "Dr. Reiner, if I don't go into the Army now, they'll put me in jail!"

Reiner protested by saying, "I'll call the President!"

Needless to say, Reiner didn't call the President, but he was very upset. Fortunately, Breines learned of a program under which he would only have to serve six months on active duty instead of two years. The catch was that he would have to enter the active Army Reserves and commit to serve for a number of years thereafter. That would require him to report for periodic drills in the evening and attend summer camp for a month each year for a number of years. But, it was still better than being away for two years.

The new arrangement was intended to allow him to remain in the Symphony. In those days, there was only a twenty-eight week winter season and six weeks during the summer. Breines was able to arrange being away for six months during the summer and to return in the autumn when the new season was to begin. But then a new problem arose. When Breines returned to Chicago from his six months of Army service, he came down with pneumonia and was unable to return to the Symphony. He missed the opening of the winter season and the first few weeks thereafter. Reiner was highly offended by his absence. One would think Breines had intentionally caught pneumonia just to offend Reiner.

Reiner never forgave Breines for what he believed was his untimely absence. From that moment on, he began picking on Breines with predictable results. I was very upset as well, because Breines was a wonderful percussionist and good friend, and I wanted him to stay with the orchestra. But his relationship with Reiner continued to deteriorate for the rest of that season. At its end, Breines chose to resign and return to New York.

As it turned out, leaving the Chicago Symphony was the best move Breines had ever made, careerwise. Upon returning to New York, he immediately found work in the orchestras of Broadway's most prestigious theaters. He soon had so many students, he had to secure a special studio to accommodate them. Eventually, he remarried and opened up a music store and school in Deer Park, Long Island that became very successful. It is still in operation and he is without doubt a millionaire today and very happy.

As for the rest of us who were left behind, we continued to endure the ravages of Reiner's antisocial behavior as well as make do with a very unhappy workplace, generally. We were not only abused but underpaid as well. Collectively, the musicians of the Chicago Symphony Orchestra had absolutely nothing to say about their pay and working conditions. The only part of our work life that made it all bearable was the fact that so many of Reiner's concerts, as well as those of other stellar guest conductors, were very artistically satisfying. We continued to make many wonderful recordings, which along with our telecasts and radio broadcasting were building a far-flung reputation of musical excellence. Our audiences, which were now international as well as domestic, were bringing pressure to bear for more touring. These CSO fans wanted to see and hear the orchestra in live performances.

Occasionally, the Chicago Symphony did do some minor touring, but not in the world-class venues necessary to establish this orchestra as one of the greatest on the planet. While building that reputation, Reiner was also doing his usual best to alienate some musical soloists of world-class stature.

One of the worst episodes occurred during the recording of a planned set of disks for RCA featuring Artur Rubenstein, one of the most famous and beloved piano artists alive. The project, entitled *The Concerto*, called for us to record the Rachmaninoff Second Piano Concerto and his Variations on a Theme of Paganini, the Grieg A Minor Concerto for Piano and another concerto yet to be decided.

Despite the stature of Rubenstein, Reiner considered himself to be in complete charge of this project. We successfully recorded the Rachmaninoff Variations, but the sessions devoted to the Second Piano Concerto were another story. There loomed a classic confrontation of two titans.

Rubenstein had a very flamboyant style of playing the piano with showy movements of his arms through space. Occasionally, this style of playing caused Rubinstein to hit a few minor "clinkers", or wrong notes. In live performances, these were passed off as part of his particular grand style. But playing any clinkers at all in a recording was just unacceptable to Rubenstein because such mistakes would be preserved for posterity and not soon forgotten.

He was having a particularly difficult time with one of the technically demanding passages in the Concerto, continually requesting that the passage be done over and over again until the piano solo was technically perfect. Finally, these demands got to Reiner's ego. Reiner suddenly rapped his baton on his music stand, and in an angry fit, refused to make any additional intercuts. He said, "No. No more. We cannot be held responsible for the mistakes of the soloist." He was asking for the same technical perfection from Rubenstein that he had always demanded of his own musicians. It had to be done right the first time, or else!

Reiner called for an intermission. The tension was nearly palpable. While listening to some of the playbacks, one could see that Rubenstein, sitting next to a silent and stone-faced Reiner, was very close to tears. He was doing everything in his power to not completely break down. We did manage to finish the two Rachmaninoff pieces, but the rest of the project was scrapped. Rubenstein completed the project with Alfred Wallenstein and the Los Angeles Philharmonic. Reiner and Rubenstein, from that time on, never worked with each other again.

Everyone in the orchestra was very angry with Reiner and the manner in which he had treated Rubenstein. Not only did the musicians know about Reiner's uncontrollable temper, it seems that every orchestra member's family did as well.

On one occasion when my wife Charlotte and our eldest son, Don, attended one of our rehearsals at Orchestra Hall, even my eight-year-old son made a very profound statement about Reiner. He was sitting with his mother at the back of Orchestra Hall after the rehearsal ended, waiting for me to pack up my instruments and join them. Just as I did so, George Kuyper, the manager of the orchestra, happened to walk by. Noticing my son sitting there, he asked who this young man was. I introduced them, and wanting to make some conversation, Kuyper asked my son if he wanted to play with the Chicago Symphony some day after he grew up.

My son pondered that question for a moment and then said, "Well, maybe by the time I grow up, Reiner will be dead!" With that, Kuyper tilted his head and rolled his eyes in glee.

"I wonder what he meant by that?" Kuyper queried, knowing the answer full well. He departed without another word. It was some time until we again took my son to another rehearsal. But, he had unwittingly articulated what many in the orchestra felt.

Some of the orchestra's musicians were actually deathly afraid of Reiner and made an art form out of being as inconspicuous as possible. There was a veteran member of the First Violins, whom I first became aware of in my third season in the CSO. We were on the chartered train the orchestra took to Milwaukee one Monday afternoon when I noticed a man sitting next to the window across the aisle from us.

I asked my friend who that was, because this train had been chartered for the CSO. I inquired, "Doesn't that guy know this is a chartered train? There aren't supposed to be any 'civilians' on board!"

My friend answered, "Oh, he's a member of the orchestra. He belongs here!"

I said, "What?! I've never seen him before."

"Yeah, he manages to hide out pretty good. That's Charlie Zika. He's a Violinist." I was simply flabbergasted because I thought I already knew everyone in the orchestra.

By the summer of 1958, I met the percussionist that was to replace Breines in our section, Al Payson. When I met him, I was not yet aware that Reiner had hired him on the basis of several recordings he had heard of the Louisville Orchestra, of which our newest percussionist had been a member. They were recordings of modern American works that featured a great deal of percussion. Reiner was very impressed by the percussion playing in these recordings and hired Payson, sight unseen, to join the orchestra in the autumn.

Payson showed up unexpectedly one summer afternoon at Ravinia Park where the Chicago Symphony performs its outdoor concerts for the Ravinia Festival. He was apparently been hired by Hancock to play as an extra in the percussion section for the concert we were to perform that evening. Even Ross, who had temporarily been advanced to Principal of our section, had never met him before. The only equipment Payson brought with him was a bag of matched pairs of Triangle beaters of various weights.

Although I had never met Payson before, I was very impressed by the fact that someone who was only going to play a Triangle part with us could be so meticulous about his beaters. He was very shy and introverted, so it took some time to really know him. He was not one to tell you what was on his mind, so it often became necessary to figure that out by yourself.

I soon found out that he was that meticulous about everything he did. He was always thoroughly prepared and very cooperative with Ross and me. He joined the orchestra full-time in the autumn, and the three of us in the section became very close on a professional level. Although Payson was shy, we soon learned that he was a very warm person and easy to get along with.

It was not just with the percussion section that Reiner had problems. Edward Metzenger, the CSO's Timpanist since 1932, was constantly being criticized by Reiner. In his mind's eye, Reiner was always comparing the sound of the Timpani he wanted and that being produced by Metzenger. If Reiner had his choice, he would have brought Saul Goodman, the legendary Timpanist of the New York Philharmonic, to Chicago. Reiner had made many free lance recordings with Goodman in New York and loved his playing. The possibility of convincing Goodman to come to Chicago was slim to none. Begrudgingly, Reiner learned to tolerate Metzenger's playing, but he never learned to like it.

During Payson's first season in the orchestra, the CSO made a very prestigious tour of the important music centers in the eastern part of the country. Included in that tour were concerts in Rochester, New York, where we played in the Eastman Theater, Symphony Hall in Boston and Carnegie Hall in New York. In Rochester, we visited with Gordon Peters, whom we had learned was about to join the orchestra the following year as Principal of our section. A decision had been made by Reiner that we needed four rather than just three percussionists in our section. Peters, a Chicagoan known to Hancock and to John Weicher, the Concertmaster, was completing his work for a graduate degree at the Eastman School of Music while playing with the Rochester Philharmonic.

I can still remember the maple trees that lined the streets of Rochester where Peters lived because they were all resplendent in their golden autumn colors. It was a beautiful time of the year to be touring. The flight into Boston was equally memorable because the skies were clear and we had a spectacular view of the foliage below with its many changing hues.

Upon our arrival in Boston and checking into our hotel, Payson, Fred Wickstrom, an extra percussionist who made the tour with us, and I immediately looked into buying tickets for a play that evening since no concert was scheduled until the following day. It turned out that a play entitled *Once More With Feeling* was playing in Boston. We had heard that it was loosely based on a story about a Reiner-like orchestra conductor and his comical adventures. Apparently, we were not the only orchestra people with the desire to view this play. We met many of our colleagues there, all with the same idea. The play was especially funny particularly because we could observe these adventures in a completely detached way. We all needed that relief from the cares of our daily life.

All of us were really primed for our Boston concert, which featured Strauss's *Ein Heldenleben*. Here we were in the home of the venerated Boston Symphony Orchestra where we knew that our orchestra would be compared to their own. Apparently, Reiner felt as we did because that evening, he conducted one of the greatest concerts he had ever done in his entire career. There was a sense about it that we all experienced; it was the concert of a lifetime and we all knew it.

The concert brought down the house, with everyone in Boston's Symphony Hall applauding, cheering, whistling and yelling for what seemed like forever. The critics' reviews the next morning were ecstatic! We had come to Boston and won the hearts of all those who were there. There was a feeling of exhilaration among the orchestra members unlike any we had ever experienced before. None of us who were there would ever forget that performance, regardless of what we had to put up with to achieve it.

Our concert at New York's Carnegie Hall was also a great concert but not quite up to the level of our Boston appearance. It was, however, good enough to set all the musical tongues wagging. Prior to having heard the CSO with Reiner, many New Yorkers believed that nothing west of the Hudson River would ever compare to what they had in New York. They were singing a different tune now.

For several years before the success of our eastern tour, but unbeknown to the members of our orchestra, plans were being made for the CSO at the U.S. Department of State for a grand tour of Europe the following year. That tour, to be undertaken under a new cultural exchange agreement with the Soviet Union, was to be eleven weeks in length. Six of those weeks were supposed to be in the USSR and the remainder in Western Europe. This was an unprecedented tour for an American orchestra and would have placed the Chicago Symphony Orchestra at the forefront of the world's orchestras. Perhaps suffering with Reiner had its rewards after all. Everyone was really thrilled about the prospects of this tour and the position it would place our orchestra in on the world stage.

Nonetheless, there was a malaise present among the musicians that just wouldn't go away. It had to do with the fact that we exercised no control whatever over our own worklives. We were completely powerless and subject to the whims of others. The entire contract between The Orchestral Association, the governing body of the CSO, and our union, the Chicago Federation of Musicians, Local 10 of the American Federation of Musicians, consisted of one typewritten page. We had nothing whatever to do with the contract's negotiation, nor did we have the right to ratify whatever it was that the union had negotiated on our behalf, as meager as it may have been.

Our local union, which held only one membership meeting a year, was presided over by the infamous James Caesar Petrillo. He had been President of Local 10 since 1922 and concurrently President of the AFM from 1940 to 1958. Petrillo had given up the AFM presidency only after a scandalous trial in Los Angeles involving the musicians who made the soundtracks for motion pictures. Members of Los Angeles Local 47 had revolted against Petrillo's rule and broken away from the AFM and formed their own union.

Dr. Eric Oldberg, a wealthy and politically well-connected neurosurgeon, headed The Orchestral Association. We all knew that Petrillo and Oldberg were close friends and that Oldberg actually dictated all the terms and conditions of our contract. Each of these two men was an autocrat in his own right. All that was necessary to seal the contract between them was a handshake. The following day, the signed contract would be posted on the company bulletin board. A locked panel of glass covered the bulletin board. The only consideration the union received, as far as we knew, was the union dues of every musician in the orchestra. The payment of dues had always been a condition of employment.

After having played in Boston and meeting with some of the musicians there after our concert, we learned that conditions in that orchestra were somewhat different from our own. To begin with, Boston's orchestra was not represented by the AFM until 1940. There was a tradition there that had a committee of orchestra members bargaining with management over the terms and conditions of their contract. That tradition is still carried on today despite affiliating with the AFM.

When Petrillo was elected AFM President in 1940, one of his first priorities was the unionization of the Boston Symphony Orchestra. At the time, Boston was the only non-union major orchestra in America. Petrillo was obsessed with bringing the Boston Symphony into the AFM. When the governing body of that orchestra refused to cave in to Petrillo's demands, Petrillo unleashed a three-pronged attack that was intended to change their minds. First of all, he banned all AFM members from performing with the Boston orchestra. Since most soloists and guest conductors were also AFM members, they could no longer appear with the Boston Symphony.

Next, he banned all recording companies having contracts with the AFM, from recording the Boston Symphony. That brought a halt to the BSO's recording work and cut off a valuable source of revenue to the orchestra.

Finally, he forbade all concert halls at which AFM members performed from permitting the Boston Symphony to appear there. This cut off all touring for the orchestra. It was not too long before the Boston Symphony Trustees capitulated and quietly entered into a contract with the Boston Local of the AFM. However, the right to negotiate their own contract was retained by the Orchestra Committee.

The Boston Committee had the naive notion that most unionized orchestras negotiated their own contracts and were surprised to learn that such was not the case in Chicago. Just as the musicians had nothing to say about the unionization of the Boston Symphony in 1940, the Chicago musicians had nothing to say about their own contracts in 1958. All Petrillo was interested in as far as unionizing the Boston Symphony was concerned was the collection of union dues from these musicians. Other demands came later. The fact that the Boston Symphony musicians had not previously paid tribute to the union was anathema to Petrillo.

But now, eighteen years later, when Petrillo was no longer the head of the AFM, and no longer had the power he had in 1940 because the tactics used then were now banned by law, Petrillo somehow became more vulnerable. The fear that this man instilled in musicians began to wane.

Chapter 3

The Sad State of the Arts

It was not just the musicians of the Boston Symphony and their counterparts in Chicago that were suffering from short seasons and low pay. In the late 1950's, all of America's symphony orchestras were suffering economically, if not artistically. In some orchestras, valued musicians were leaving their jobs for better paying ones, both in and out of the music industry. Orchestra boards were accumulating deficits that threatened the very existence of these cultural institutions.

The situation was so grave that the U.S. Congress convened hearings on the plight of these organizations and their employees. George Zazofsky, a veteran violinist with the Boston Symphony Orchestra, testified that musicians could not afford to continue in their chosen profession. When asked what it would take to help musicians stay at their jobs, Zazofsky replied that if musicians could earn even as little as $100 a week all year long, that would be very helpful. He thought that musicians should be earning the kind of living that college professors were.

In addition to all the problems that working in the CSO under Reiner entailed, it was the short season in Chicago that really frustrated the musicians. Even though working under Reiner was unpleasant for the most part, at least it meant that you were being paid to perform music at the time. In Chicago, there were two separate and distinct seasons in which one worked. The winter season, which ran for twenty eight weeks, and the summer season that ran for six weeks. That left eighteen weeks, more than four months, in which we were totally unemployed. And there was no unemployment compensation to help smooth the bridge between seasons.

Since these seasons were operated by two different legal entities, they had separate contracts with the union whose pay and working conditions were not the same. The Ravinia Festival Association in Highland Park operated the summer season, while The Orchestral Association in Chicago's downtown ran the winter season. These associations did cooperate with each other for the most part, but not on all matters. The Orchestral Association's Board of Trustees was, for the most part, old time Chicago wealth, mainly Protestant. The Ravinia Board was primarily newer North Shore wealth, mainly Jewish. Each organization had a separate Music Director, management, and staff with differing artistic policies.

Much earlier in its history, the Chicago Symphony Orchestra's musicians were mainly German and Czech Gentiles. The only Jews were in the Violin and Viola sections. When we joined the orchestra in October 1954, James Ross and I

15

were the first Jews in the orchestra who were not string players. Reiner, although born a Jew, had converted to Roman Catholicism, probably for business reasons. But the same could be said for many of the great conductors of the day.

The Congressional response to the economic plights of America's performing arts institutions was the creation of the following federally funded foundations that were authorized to make grants to performing institutions: the National Endowment for the Arts and its counterpart in the Humanities.

The non-profit corporations that operated symphony orchestras did not welcome these Endowments initially. They feared that money from the federal government would have too many strings attached. (No pun intended.) They were very much afraid that bureaucrats in Washington would be dictating artistic policy. It smelled too much like the Communist Commissars that ran the cultural institutions of the Soviet Union, and they wanted no part of it. After many assurances that such oversight was not going to be a factor, these institutions reluctantly accepted government grants as part of their fund-raising efforts.

Even before any of these orchestras applied for a government grant, the Ford Foundation announced a massive program of grants to help put a solid base under most of America's major orchestras.

These programs, which can be called *socialism for the wealthy*, had virtually no impact whatever on the economic conditions of individual musicians or the length of orchestra seasons. We continued to live lives of quiet desperation.

In the meanwhile, plans were going forward for the State Department sponsored tour, which was to begin in the spring of 1959. The CSO's musicians and their families were also making many plans. There had never been such a long tour anywhere by the orchestra. Because six weeks of the tour were to be in the Soviet Union, special plans had to be made to accommodate the anticipated lack of consumer goods we have come to take for granted. Peters, our new section Principal, was planning to join the orchestra before the tour began. He was waiting for word about the special rehearsals that would precede our embarkation.

What no one had any inkling of was the current condition of Reiner's health. Although only 71 years of age, he was already suffering the ravages of congestive heart failure. His doctors advised him that the rigors of an eleven-week tour, particularly considering the unknown travel conditions in the USSR, were beyond his capacity and would pose a major threat to his health. But this information was known only to Reiner.

Suddenly, and without warning, the musicians of the Chicago Symphony were informed by a terse bulletin on the company board, that our long anticipated tour of Europe had been canceled by Reiner, who suddenly informed management that he refused to go on this tour. That occurred just six weeks before we were scheduled to leave. It is difficult to describe the utter doom and gloom felt by every member of our orchestra. We felt betrayed! No conversation held that fateful day in Orchestra Hall omitted a discussion of Reiner's betrayal. Our anticipated moment of triumph turned into ashes before our eyes. The rumor was that Reiner had said that it rained that time of year in Moscow.

Reiner was absent from Orchestra Hall that week and a guest conductor was directing the subscription concerts. That was just as well, because there was no telling what might have happened if he were actually there.

At the intermission of the Thursday evening concert, one of the musicians laid an old formal tailcoat on the floor of the locker room and placed an old battered baton on it. It was meant as an effigy of Reiner, and nearly everyone there trampled all over that effigy to vent his or her anger. The news of the incident was reported in *Time* magazine along with the story of the tour's cancellation.

Officials at the State Department were stunned by Reiner's refusal to go on the tour. With so little time left before it was to begin, they turned to Leonard Bernstein and the New York Philharmonic as viable substitutes. To cancel the tour altogether would have been a severe diplomatic blow to U.S./Soviet relations, which were in a delicate state of deténte.

Before the musicians' tempers had time to cool, Walter Hancock, the Personnel Manager, announced during a rehearsal intermission that there was to be a meeting of all the musicians in the chorus room immediately following the rehearsal. As we all assembled, no one was quite sure what was going to happen next. Hancock soon ended the speculation.

He told the assembled musicians that Reiner had been humiliated by the story in *Time* magazine of the trampling of his effigy in the locker room. He demanded an immediate collective apology from the orchestra's musicians. (We were still unaware at that time of Reiner's health problems and the true reason for his refusal to take the tour.)

Suddenly, I was struck by the irony of Reiner's demand. He was doing all these terrible things to us, and he was the one who was demanding an apology. Without thinking of the consequences, I suddenly broke the stunned silence that hung over the chorus room while Hancock was waiting to see what our reaction would be.

In an unusually calm voice considering the turmoil that was going on inside my head, I said, "Walter, there isn't going to be any apology. If anyone is going to apologize here, it's going to be Dr. Reiner to us!" Before the sound of my last word had a chance to die out, the orchestra members burst into spontaneous applause and cheering. It was the first time in the history of the Chicago Symphony Orchestra that anyone had ever told off the Music Director and the Personnel Manager. The musicians were absolutely euphoric!

But, once the words were out of my mouth, I briefly reflected on what had just happened. What now? Hancock just threw up his hands, and suddenly, the meeting was over. The musicians were all over me. From a mild mannered anonymous member of the percussion section, in a single moment, I was converted into the musicians' hero who really told the powers that are what the musicians really felt like. They felt great relief that the management finally had some idea of the pain we were suffering.

Even George Kuyper, the orchestra's manager, was angry with Reiner. He had been working with officials at the State Department for three years to settle all the details of the tour. It had all been for naught. He was so discouraged that when the opportunity came a few years later to move to Los Angeles to manage the Philharmonic, he jumped at the opportunity and left Chicago forever.

What had happened in the chorus room at Orchestra Hall that day in the spring of 1959 started a chain of events that had a life of its own. From that day on, musicians were suddenly emboldened to do something to change their worklives. They were no longer content to have others make all the decisions that affected their lives. One of the first things that occurred to them was the formation of their own elected orchestra committee. They weren't quite sure just how to proceed. The idea suddenly floated was that the musicians should go over to the union and see Petrillo en masse to demand permission to form an orchestra committee.

Arrangements were made to walk over to the union's headquarters on West Washington Street on a Thursday afternoon immediately after the morning rehearsal. We knew that the union's Board of Directors held their meeting every Thursday and that Petrillo was likely to be there.

When we all arrived at the union's headquarters, it was like a landing force engaged in an invasion. We all trudged up the two flights of stairs to the reception area of the Board Room and demanded to see Petrillo. We were admitted to the Board Room, which was yet another flight of stairs up, where the only officers remaining were the elderly and diminutive David Katz, who was also the union's attorney and always wore a fedora hat, Leo Nye, the Recording Secretary, who was also an attorney and former Field Officer for the National Labor Relations Board, and Petrillo himself.

Petrillo, who had obviously been informed that we were coming and why, asked us what the problem was? It was Ray Still, the orchestra's Principal Oboe, who answered. He made no bones about the fact that we wanted to form our own committee like the musicians of the Boston Symphony had.

Petrillo pretended not to know about the committee in Boston and badgered us with all sorts of questions. He also made a long speech in which he warned us not to engage in "dual-unionism." After a frank discussion that lasted more than an hour, he reluctantly agreed to let us form a committee that was to act as liaison between the orchestra management, the orchestra members and the union.

Of course, we could have formed a committee of our members whether Petrillo gave us permission or not. We just thought it more prudent at the time to not look for more problems than we already had.

As it turned out, the Congress was also holding hearings on the undemocratic practices of labor unions and the shady dealings of labor relations consultants who were acting as bag men. By October of 1959, Congress passed legislation sponsored by Congressmen Landrum and Griffin called the Labor-Management Reporting and Disclosure Act of 1959. It provided a Bill of Rights for union members and mandated the holding of democratic elections of officers as well as the maximum term that could be served between elections. Labor organizations were also required to make annual disclosure reports of their finances that were available to the public. As it turned out, the timing of this legislation's passage could not have been better.

The musicians promptly held an election for an orchestra committee. It was decided that nine members would make a good representative number. We named our committee the Chicago Symphony Orchestra Members' Committee and the organization of musicians as the Chicago Symphony Orchestra Members' Society. Harry Sturm, the Assistant Principal 'Cello, was elected its first Chairman and Robert Alexa, a Violist, was elected Secretary. Alexa was empowered to draft a set of by-laws by which we could operate.

Harry Sturm, a friendly and non-controversial musician, turned out to be a poor choice for Chairman. He did not provide the kind of leadership the committee needed at the time of its formation. He was very conservative and could not provide the ideas and set the goals the musicians desperately required. As we learned the following year, he didn't have the strength of character we were looking for either.

Although Petrillo had approved the formation of the committee, he certainly wasn't happy about it. Such committees always represented a threat to established unions because there was always the possibility that such a group would eventually seek to take the exclusive rights to bargain a contract away from it. That would mean that the flow of members' dues into the union's coffers would come to an end. It was not only the union that felt threatened by the committee's formation.

Dr. Eric Oldberg, President of The Orchestral Association, was also very upset by this turn of events. He was an autocratic individual who was used to being completely in charge of every activity he was engaged in. In fact, when he was elected to head the orchestra's Board of Trustees, he told the other Trustees that he would only serve as long as there was a unanimous Board behind him.

Even the nurses who worked for him at the hospital where he operated on peoples' brains were afraid of and intimidated by him.

As the Members' Committee became more organized, their activities were closely monitored by both Oldberg and Petrillo. These men felt a common threat in the activities of the Committee. They had been used to amicably deciding between the two of them just what was to be in the contract that governed the orchestra's labor matters. Now, that arrangement was being threatened. They knew in time that they would have to deal directly with the musicians' representatives and probably with their lawyer as well. They didn't like the prospects one bit.

They were in no mood to voluntarily agree to this new arrangement. They knew that they would have to devise a strategy to nip this new labor activism in the bud. For now, they would wait and see how things developed.

But develop they did. It became obvious that the committee was in need of an attorney's advice. Those of us on the committee were all neophytes and totally ignorant of labor law and procedures. Although the committee did develop a dues structure that most of the musicians were willing to comply with, it would take some time to accumulate a nest egg. Fortunately, one of the musicians had a connection that could arrange for the committee to receive some *pro bono* advice. We got top-notch advice from one of the best labor lawyers in the business, Abner Mikva.

At the time, Mikva was a partner in the Chicago labor law firm of Goldberg, Mikva and Shadur. The "Goldberg" was Arthur Goldberg, General Counsel of the SteelWorkers Union and soon to become the U.S. Secretary of Labor. He eventually was nominated to and served on the U.S. Supreme Court.

The connection was that Arthur Goldberg, from Chicago's South Side, was married to a woman whose sister was the wife of Sheppard Lehnhoff, a Violist in the Chicago Symphony and staunch supporter of the Members' Committee.

Of course, Mikva, always well connected politically, eventually became a Member of Congress. Later, he was appointed to one of the most important judicial posts in the nation, a Justice of the United States Court of Appeals for the District of Columbia. That is the court that rules on the constitutionality of the laws passed by Congress. He longed served as its Chief Justice before resigning to accept a post as Counselor to the President of the United States. Milton Shadur is currently a Senior Judge of the U.S. District Court for the Northern District of Illinois.

We met regularly with Mikva in his Chicago Loop office, and he gave us sage advice on how to organize the members of the orchestra and accomplish what we collectively wanted to do. One of our first goals was to win the right to ratify our contracts.

The whole notion of labor activism within the orchestra was not readily accepted by all its members. There was a vocal minority of musicians who thought that what we were going was all wrong. They were content to let management run the show as they pleased. There were a variety of reasons for this opposition. Some thought it was beneath the dignity of artists to act like common laborers. Others, including some of the Principal players, thought we just didn't have the right to tell our employers how our workplace ought to be run. It was clear that the Committee had its work cut out for it.

Through a number of freewheeling meetings, members freely spoke of the goals they thought we should go after. They were well aware that we would be opposed by management and by the union as well.

Chapter 4

The Plot

Gradually, we were winning the support of some of the minority of musicians that had opposed what the Committee was doing. Primarily the number of rank and file musicians who firmly supported the goals of the Members' Committee won over these musicians. The fact that our support was growing set off alarm bells in Union headquarters and in the office of Dr. Eric Oldberg, President of The Orchestral Association..

Oldberg contacted Petrillo to arrange for a secret meeting to plot a strategy to stop this movement while it was still young and had not yet gained momentum. Their meeting took place at an undisclosed Loop location at which they mutually agreed that it was necessary to cooperate in order to squelch this committee of "Young Turks." Oldberg thought that if the most vocal and active members of the orchestra could be fired, it would throw the "Fear of God" into the orchestra. Petrillo agreed and offered to hold off any help the fired musicians might ask of the union until it was too late to file Unfair Labor Practice charges with the National Labor Relations Board. Once the six-month limitation had passed, Petrillo would then say that there was nothing he could do, although he had tried his best. That would have foreclosed any chance of reinstatement by order of the NLRB.

Of course, what they were plotting may have been illegal, but not criminal. Whether that plot was even illegal would depend on whether the NLRB would assert jurisdiction over symphony orchestras. Without jurisdiction, the case would be moot, and the Labor Board had not yet spoken to the issue. Apparently, their respective attorneys had briefed both Oldberg and Petrillo on the law. If they had not, they would have been risking a great deal of embarassment, at a minimum.

Now that the plot had been hatched, it would be necessary to pinpoint those whose firings would have the greatest impact on the orchestra. Obviously, artistic considerations were not a factor. No one had ever been fired from the Chicago Symphony previously for having engaged in a concerted action for the mutual aid and benefit of the employees. Those were the types of employee activities that were supposed to protected by the National Labor Relations Act.

Since Dr. Oldberg, as the Chief Executive Officer of the Symphony's Governing Board, had access to more information about the musicians than the union had, he was up to him to decide which musicians were to be targeted for dismissal. Normally, it was the Music Director who made the decisions relating to the hiring and firing of the musicians. However, stopping the spread of union activity within the orchestra was deemed more important than any artistic consideration.

Oldberg determined that the five most vocal and active musicians involved in this unprecedented activity should be terminated. He asked Walter Hancock, the Personnel Manager, for assistance in designating the five employees, but Hancock wisely begged off. He said that if it were ever learned that he was involved in this decision, he would no longer have the credibility he needed to perform his regular functions.

That was when Oldberg determined to go directly to the most reliable source for this information. He quietly communicated with Harry Sturm, the Chairman of the Members' Committee, asking whether he would meet with him some evening at the University Club, and Sturm accepted the invitation. In his naiveté, Sturm thought he could make some progress for the Committee's acceptance in such a private meeting. He didn't know what Oldberg had in mind.

When the meeting took place, Dr. Oldberg railed against the formation of a committee in the orchestra and told Sturm that this was the worst possible thing the orchestra members could be doing. After all, hadn't The Orchestral Association always taken care of the "important" members of the orchestra? He was referring to the section Principals and Assistant Principals, of which Sturm was one.

He convinced Sturm that it was in the best long-term interest of the orchestra to put an end to this activity immediately. He then asked for Sturm's cooperation in naming the five most vocal and active musicians that were involved in this horrible activity. Sturm finally agreed with Oldberg and gave him the five names he sought. They were William York and Robert Coleman, Violists, Samuel Siegel, a Violinist, Rudolph Nashan, Trumpet, and yours truly. The musicians didn't learn about this meeting until some months later. One of the Committee members had a source on the administrative staff who provided the information. Dr. Oldberg had unwittingly let the information leak out because he was so proud of what he had done.

It was in the spring of 1960 that the five of us who had been marked for professional extinction learned of our fate. We simply received the *pro forma* notice of non-renewal that musicians normally received when being let go for artistic reasons. The word of these notices spread through the orchestra like wildfire. The opinion of the orchestra was divided because Dr. Reiner's role in these notices was not yet known. Some of the musicians were just outraged while others were simply fearful. There was an immediate sense that these notices had nothing whatever to do with how these five members performed as musicians, but was in retaliation for their union activity, which was precisely what Oldberg and Petrillo wanted.

It was necessary to determine at the outset just what Dr. Reiner's role was in the distribution of the notices. Ray Still, Principal Oboe, and Leonard Sharrow, Principal Bassoon, both avid supporters of the Committee, decided to confront Reiner. They marched uninvited into Dr. Reiner's dressing room behind the stage of Orchestra Hall after the rehearsal. Ray Still was the first to speak and he wasted no time in getting right to the heart of the matter.

"Dr. Reiner, why are these five people being let go?"

Reiner was shocked that these two musicians had been so blunt. He asked, "What five people?"

Still and Sharrow ticked off the names of the five musicians who had received notices.

Reiner looked concerned. "Well, I did have some musicians in mind to let go at the end of the season, but none of these. They're some of my best people!" Reiner was genuinely angry that others were making what he thought was his decision to make. He still didn't know why these five musicians had been targeted. In the end, Reiner had no role in this episode, and neither could he be counted upon to come to the aid of these musicians.

As Petrillo had predicted, the Committee made a date to meet with him at his union headquarters. While the first meeting with Petrillo had been in the union's Board Room, this meeting took place in his office on the top floor of the union's building. This was the inner sanctum in which very few of the union's members had ever been.

It was a large room with Oriental carpets and a huge carved desk in one corner. The windows were reputedly made of bulletproof glass. The office's door had a lead plate in it and many locks. Next to the office was a smaller room that could be used as living quarters. It had a leather couch and a bathroom complete with shower.

Again, Petrillo feigned ignorance of the reason the Committee had come to see him. He was then briefed on the notices that had been distributed to the five musicians and was asked to meet with Dr. Oldberg to convince him that the notices should be rescinded.

Petrillo asked, "Are you sure that these people don't deserve the notices because maybe they aren't up to the standards of the orchestra?" Again, he was pretending not to know of the true reasons for the notices. He was assured that was not the case and was told of the conversation Still and Sharrow had had with Reiner. He still looked skeptical.

Finally, he agreed to talk to his "good friend, Dr. Oldberg" at the "propitious" moment. We all thought that was a strange word for Petrillo to use because we knew he had never gone past the fourth grade in elementary school. But he used it again. "When the propitious time comes, I'll talk to him about it." With the commitment made, we thanked him and left his office.

Weeks went by without a word from Petrillo. One of the Committee members was assigned the job of phoning Petrillo at the union to see what was going on. The answer was always the same; the propitious time to speak to Dr. Oldberg about this matter had not yet arrived.

The Committee met with a number of well known Chicago labor leaders to seek their advice on our predicament. One of the most helpful was Sidney Lens, a long time activist with the Service Employees International Union. Lens was known for having rid the Chicago Elevator Operators Union of Al Capone's hoodlums in earlier times, and had lived to tell the tale. He has also written many books on labor matters.

None of the labor leaders we contacted had anything good to say about Petrillo and the musicians union. Petrillo had never honored any other union's picket lines, so in their opinion, Petrillo was nothing more than a petty crook. They all warned us to look out for our backsides where Petrillo was concerned. We heeded their advice.

As the weeks since our meeting with Petrillo stretched into months, we began to become alarmed at our prospects. The news that Petrillo had met with Dr. Oldberg on our behalf was not forthcoming. After five months had passed since the notices of non-renewal had been served, a few of us thought it was time we took matters into our own hands.

We also learned later that Edward Miller, the former attorney for The Orchestral Association, and then Chairman of the National Labor Relations Board in Washington, DC, had warned some of the Symphony's Trustees that the attempt to fire these musicians could have dire consequences for The Orchestral Association if these musicians decided to file Unfair Labor Practice charges with the NLRB.

At the time, however, we didn't know of Miller's concern. By then, we had pretty much surmised what Petrillo was up to and thought it was time for some concerted action. We began having meetings with small groups of the Orchestra's musicians in our homes. It was explained to them that Petrillo had betrayed us. It was also crucial that the five who had been targeted for dismissal had to be protected, or else no one would ever feel safe enough to speak out again in this orchestra. We asked for and got commitments from those who attended these meetings that if the matter was not resolved before six months had passed, we would all go out on an Unfair Labor Practice strike against The Orchestral Association. Strikers in such situations are protected more than ordinary "economic" strikers.

Fortunately, it never became necessary to carry out the strike we had planned. When word of our meetings got back to Orchestra Hall, it was only a matter of days when the five of us each received written notice to please "disregard" the notice of non-renewal we had received previously. No other explanation was given. As suddenly as this ill-conceived plot had been sprung, it disappeared. We had achieved a major victory. We also learned that if we could just stick together, we could achieve virtually any legitimate goal. It was a hard-learned but valuable lesson.

Eventually, because it became known that Sturm had met with Oldberg early on and had been the one who fingered the five musicians who received notice, Sturm was not reelected to the Committee. He was so disgraced that a few years later, he resigned from the Chicago Symphony to take a position with the Milwaukee Symphony Orchestra where he became the Personnel Manager.

Chapter 5

Killing the Pension

While the Members' Committee continued to consolidate its position within the Orchestra, we learned that Jimmy Petrillo had some new plans of his own. He knew that we had upset the plans made with Dr. Oldberg. Perhaps he was able to see the handwriting on the wall and surmised that his days as President of the Chicago Local were coming to a close much in the same way as his days as International President had ended earlier.

At the next annual meeting of the Chicago Federation of Musicians in October, we learned that a resolution was to be voted upon to grant Petrillo a pension that would be payable after he was no longer President of the Local. That pension was to equal the salary he was now receiving as President, $500 weekly, a pretty substantial sum at that time.

This could serve as our opportunity to show Petrillo that there are consequences for betraying the people he had pledged to serve. As members of the union, we were helping to pay his salary while he was plotting with our employer to punish us for exercising our rights. Of course, that wasn't what union presidents were supposed to be doing, and we were very upset with Petrillo. Pensions are sometimes viewed as a reward for an outstanding worklife, but we didn't believe Petrillo was entitled to a pension. Besides, we knew that even while receiving a salary of $500 weekly as our Local's President, he had somehow managed to become a millionaire. One can only speculate about how that was accomplished.

We solicited meetings with other members of the union who were not members of the Symphony whom we thought may be sympathetic to our cause. They were told of Petrillo's treachery with the members of the Symphony and were asked if they would cooperate with us to deny Petrillo his pension. We were surprised at the number of members who were against Petrillo and agreed to help us. We started to study the union's by-laws in earnest and familiarize ourselves with *Roberts' Rules of Order*, the primer on parliamentary procedure. We didn't want to be outfoxed at the meeting.

One of our most committed allies was a Violinist who doubled on Trumpet by the name of Marvin Rochetti. He worked primarily in the free lance field, performing with many large dance orchestras that worked in the big hotels downtown. He seemed to know just about everyone in the music business, and he hated Petrillo with a passion. That hatred proved to be valuable in the future.

We knew from past experience that Petrillo and his allies would have every old crony of theirs who was a member at that meeting. It was our job to organize the opposition within the Local. These activities now occupied most of our spare time. From orchestral musicians, we were learning how to become political operatives.

The Members' Committee started holding their meetings to plan strategies and discuss other concerns while having breakfast before the morning orchestra rehearsals would begin. We would meet around a large circular table at Miller's Pub on Adams Street and Wabash Avenue. There was nowhere in Orchestra Hall that we felt secure. The table was set in a corner of the popular restaurant under a large Tiffany light fixture and was a very congenial environment. Fortunately, the restaurant did most of its business at lunch and dinner. We therefore had all the privacy we needed in the early morning hours.

At that time, Chicago Local 10, AFM, had about 11,000 white musicians as members. Black musicians had their own segregated Local, 208. The Chicago Symphony's personnel were still lily white, through no fault of ours. It was with the white local union of musicians, after all, that The Orchestral Association had a contract. That was by design, not circumstance.

The vast majority of Local 10 members were part-time musicians who were fortunate to find an occasional weekend in which to work as a musician. Primarily, these part-time musicians made their livelihoods at other, non-musical, jobs. Many of these part-timers were not a concern to us because in all probability, they would not attend the annual meeting. We were more concerned about those part-time musicians whom had retired and could be counted upon by Petrillo to attend the annual meeting.

Those who either worked regularly as musicians, and those that had been full-time musicians but were now retired, had to be converted. There were many of these and we had our work cut out for us. The most important thing we could do was to let members know that there was a faction that intended to oppose the pension. This kind of opposition had been unheard of in our Local.

We had made our plans well, even down to the point of writing out the exact words that had to be said to properly make a motion. The words were on small pieces of paper held by designated members of our faction.

The day of the annual meeting finally arrived and we were prepared to outmaneuver and outsmart whatever plans Petrillo and his henchmen may have made. The only thing we couldn't do was to change the date of the meeting. It was held on a day in which we had two rehearsals scheduled. If the meeting ran too long, we would have to leave the meeting in order to make the rehearsal on time.

Petrillo had also done some strategic planning. His operatives had appealed to every old timer they could find to attend this meeting. He even had all the members of the American Federation of Musicians' International Executive Board there, posing as members of our Local. Of course, they were not members of our Local and were not entitled to vote at this meeting. But, they were there, regardless of the rules, to not only observe, but to vote.

Finally, at the appointed hour, with hundreds of members packed in the meeting room, Petrillo entered and all his supporters stood up and applauded. We made a point of neither rising nor applauding. Petrillo immediately saw that he was going to have a problem on his hands. He immediately announced a change in the order of business for this meeting so that the resolution on his pension would not be voted upon until the very end of the meeting. He knew that the members of the Chicago Symphony would have to leave at a certain time in order to get to their rehearsal.

One of our members immediately arose to object to the change in the order of business. He made a motion that the order of business that was printed in the notice of the meeting be adhered to. Another of our people seconded the motion. As the meeting's chairman, Petrillo was obligated to put the motion to a vote. Our motion carried, to Petrillo's surprise! He would have to use a different tactic to delay the business of the meeting as long as he could. He decided to make one of his classic speeches that could go on for what seemed like forever.

Petrillo began to recount the entire history of his time as President of the Local. Covering nearly forty years could take a very long time. He was a masterful speechmaker and could be mesmerizing when he chose to be. As he droned on and on, a few members actually arose and left the room. We soon realized that if his speech lasted too long, we would not have the opportunity to vote on the pension resolution at all.

Suddenly, Samuel Siegel, a CSO Violinist and one of the musicians who had been targeted for dismissal from the Orchestra, stood up and stopped Petrillo right in his tracks. In a very strong voice, he said, "Mr. President, I rise to a Point of Order" According to *Roberts' Rules of Order*, raising a point of order could interrupt a speaker, and must be ruled upon as soon as the Point of Order is stated.

Petrillo was dumbfounded. No one had ever interrupted one of his speeches previously. As soon as he regained his composure, he asked, "What is your Point of Order?"

"Well," said Siegel, "you've been talking for more than an hour now, and you haven't gotten past 1937 yet!" This bizarre move by Siegel startled and amused many of those in attendance. Petrillo was embarrassed and flustered! Of course, what Siegel stated was not really a Point of Order, but it served to break up the tempo of Petrillo's speech. It ended five minutes later and the meeting moved to the subject of Petrillo's pension.

A number of speakers were heard, both pro and con. As the debate continued on, it became apparent to Petrillo that he was not going to get his pension. Finally, Petrillo suggested that perhaps the money that would have been earmarked for his pension be devoted to some other worthy cause. Almost as though on cue, Lillian Poenisch, an elderly member of the Local arose and suggested that perhaps the money could be used to fund concerts by the retired members of the Local. This was readily acceptable to most of the members who were there.

While the meeting's outcome was not what we planned, it was a means of resolving the debate while not authorizing a pension for Petrillo. From that time to this, those funds have been set aside by the union to subsidize the City Symphony Orchestra, as it has come to be called. The orchestra is composed of retired members of the union who enjoy performing classical music and who receive a small stipend from the fund that was created. They rehearse every Monday morning in the same meeting room at union headquarters in which this historic debate took place. At least, Petrillo had saved face by not having the membership directly deny him a pension.

But, the bad news for Petrillo was not yet over. The coalition formed to defeat the resolution to provide a pension for Petrillo was to become the basis for other activities that played themselves out in the next few years.

Chapter 6

Working with Petrillo

Considering that James Caesar Petrillo ran the Chicago Federation of Musicians, Local 10, AFM, for nearly forty years without brooking any interference from anyone, the activities that were going on now were difficult for him to understand. Surely, Petrillo noticed the enactment of legislation on the federal level that gave union members rights and privileges they had never had before. In addition, those rights could be enforced in court or an administrative agency. It all seemed like a conspiracy to drive him from office as head of this powerful and wealthy union.

He had always taken a proprietary view of the union since becoming its President in 1922. Although it was always thought that he had some connection to the Mafia, that was never conclusively established. Surely, when he became the union's leader in the early 1920's, he operated in much the same way that the Mafioso street gangs did. The union was run just like the protection racket operated by mobsters. The real protection needed, of course, was from the mobsters.

In the prosperity enjoyed by the nation after the First World War, Petrillo wasn't busy organizing musicians who would then demand that their employers recognize and bargain with the union. His style of organizing was just the opposite. It was strictly "top down."

He would walk into a successful Chinese restaurant with a few goons, for instance, and demand to see the proprietor in his office. He would then tell the proprietor that he thought this establishment ought to have a few musicians playing here. If he was met by a refusal, he would simply place what appeared to be a bomb on the owner's desk, and then make the same request. The owner usually gave in without any further persuasion. There was soon a small orchestra playing in this establishment, all of whose members had to be in Petrillo's union. But those days were now gone forever.

He had often said that he took up the trumpet as a youth, but wasn't very good at it. That was when he decided "to go into the union business." He ran the union as though it was his own personal business. Everything he had ever done throughout the years was more for the benefit of Jimmy Petrillo than for the musicians whose dues paid his salary and provided all the other perks of his office.

He was very tough in his dealings with the union's members. Many complained that he was tougher with his members than he ever was with an employer. If any musician had a complaint and went to see Petrillo in his plush offices, the first thing he was met with was a handgun that Petrillo took out of his desk drawer and laid on the desktop. That was usually enough to discourage even the most serious complaints.

Our Members' Committee was making progress in its campaign to make alliances with other factions within the musicians' union. We had also gotten a long sought-after concession from the union. They had begrudgingly agreed to allow the orchestra the right to ratify its future contracts. They had no idea at the time how much grief that concession would cause the union.

The first time we had the opportunity to actually ratify a union contract was very early in the 1960's. The union "negotiated" a new contract with the Ravinia Festival Association that reduced both the weekly salaries paid there as well as the number of weeks worked. There was just no way that the union was able to sell this contract to the members of the Chicago Symphony Orchestra. Time after time, the union came back with the same contract, only to have it rejected by the orchestra members. In the end, Ravinia's negotiators conceded defeat and agreed to keep the contract at its current levels even though they were beginning to accumulate deficits.

Petrillo, unwittingly, was getting used to the idea of meeting with the Members' Committee in his office because we there so often. He began to feel a bit more at ease with us and actually managed to be a charming host on occasion. However, he still didn't know where Orchestra Hall was located. On the few occasions that he actually showed up there, he admitted that he had to ask the taxi driver to take him, because he simply didn't know how to get there.

While we began to socialize with him on a superficial level, we never lost sight of the fact that he was the most significant impediment to our being able to control our work lives. There were many things we needed to accomplish, and we knew that none of these would happen as long as he was President of the union.

When George Kuyper left his post as manager of the orchestra to move to Los Angeles, we were amazed that the orchestra's Trustees actually hired a young and enlightened manager by the name of Silas Edman to replace him. He was a warm, friendly individual that accepted working with our Committee as a natural part of his duties. He was more like a friend and colleague than an antagonist. We embarked on a period of labor-management relations that was as close to ideal as we could ever imagine. But alas, it didn't last very long. Somehow, we had always known that Silas Edman was too good to be true!

The following year, Seymour Raven, a former assistant music critic at *The Chicago Tribune*, replaced him. Raven was the antithesis of Edman, and completely paranoid. He made our lives miserable in every possible way he could. He barred the Members' Committee from meeting anywhere in Orchestra Hall. While the Members' Society would be allowed to meet in the chorus room of Orchestra Hall on occasion, it was usually under surveillance. He even went so far as to prohibit a group of more than three musicians from conversing with each other anywhere in Orchestra Hall.

Without realizing it, he was shoring up our support within the orchestra to plan for what we thought would be the final assault upon the union and the overthrow of Petrillo. Sometimes his attempts at surveillance were so inept as to actually be comical.

On one occasion, the Members' Society was meeting in the chorus room immediately after a morning rehearsal. One of our Committee members, Bob Alexa, our Secretary, actually observed a shadowy figure enter the darkened chorus room just before the musicians started to gather there. The figure crouched behind the piano in a very dark corner of the room. After the meeting ended, Alexa hung around to see who would emerge after all the musicians had left. It was none other than Seymour Raven!

Now, we had both a miserable Music Director and a miserable Manager. The two of them, however, didn't get along at all. When passing by Reiner's backstage dressing room, one could often hear heated discussions going on between Raven and Reiner. Because Reiner's health was beginning to fail now in a noticeable way, Raven usually prevailed in the arguments he had with Reiner.

By the end of the 1961-62 season, Reiner was no longer able to stand while conducting concerts. He sat on a high stool shielded from the public's view by a special enclosed guardrail on the podium. It became apparent that Reiner's days were numbered.

In the meanwhile, communications with the other major symphony orchestras was providing a plethora of information on wages and working conditions. We were no longer isolated from our colleagues in other parts of the nation.

Recognizing that these communications between orchestras could spell trouble for the AFM, the Federation began sponsoring a number of symposiums for symphony orchestra representatives. Delegates were invited to meet in a New York City hotel. These symposiums were presided over by AFM President Herman Kenin. He was Petrillo's handpicked successor when he stepped down as AFM President in 1958.

Kenin was a highly intelligent former lawyer and bandleader who was Petrillo's right hand man during the years Petrillo served as AFM President. At the outset, he told the delegates that these meetings would be informal and that no votes would be taken on any matter. That was taken to mean that nothing of any real substance was going to happen at these symposiums.

In the end, these symposiums were intended by the AFM only as a place where the delegates could blow off some steam. Kenin surely realized that the delegates were frustrated and wanted far more from the AFM than they got. Kenin's strategy had backfired and only served to add more fuel to the struggle to get the AFM to act like a legitimate union.

Because the delegates collectively realized that the union was not yet ready for reform, they decided to form their own independent conference. Their first meeting took place in Chicago's Roosevelt University. Most of the nation's major symphony and opera orchestras were represented. The meeting in Chicago was presided over by a Chicago Symphony Violinist, Joseph Golan.

That meeting discussed the symphony musicians' greatest needs: universal contract ratification, a communications vehicle and a comparative wage and working condition chart of the orchestras. They also agreed to meet in Cleveland within six months to formalize their organization. The decision to meet in Cleveland was made as a show of support for the embattled musicians of the Cleveland Orchestra, who were locked in an historic battle to gain the right to ratify their contracts. Their union, the Cleveland Federation of Musicians, Local 4, AFM, was even more dictatorial than Local 10 was.

When the delegates met in Cleveland, they adopted a set of by-laws as an unincorporated non-profit organization and named themselves the International Conference of Symphony & Opera Musicians (ICSOM). At the time, the conference also included Canadian orchestras who were also represented by AFM Locals. The delegates elected George Zazofsky of the Boston Symphony Orchestra as their first Chairman, and I was elected Vice Chairman. Robert Coleman, a Violist from the Chicago Symphony, was elected as Editor of its journal. Ralph (Bob) Maisel, of the St. Louis Symphony, was elected Secretary.

AFM President Kenin and the members of the International Executive Board were extremely upset by this turn of events. The idea foremost in their thinking was that ICSOM could eventually become a full-fledged labor organization and challenge the AFM for the exclusive rights to represent symphony musicians for collective bargaining purposes. If that should happen, it would represent a major blow to the financial underpinnings of the AFM because it would mean that membership dues would no longer be coming into the union's treasury.

At the time, that notion was not in anyway what ICSOM had in mind. What they really wanted was for the AFM to represent them as the symphony musicians thought they should be represented. Of course, they also wanted some respect from the AFM, which had not been forthcoming!

Chapter 7

The Election Campaign

1962 was a year that I shall never forget. A great deal has happened since that fateful year, but the events are still indelibly etched in my mind.

The 1961-62 winter season was Reiner's last as Music Director of the Chicago Symphony Orchestra. He had submitted his resignation citing failing health as the reason. He conducted less than his usual number of subscription weeks and those he did manage to conduct were with even smaller beats than his usual and legendary "vest-pocket" style of conducting. Sometimes, it simply seemed that he was leading the orchestra by sheer will, communicating what he wanted from the musicians by some mysterious form of mental telepathy.

No new Music Director was immediately named to succeed Reiner, and for an entire season, we had nothing but guest conductors. Reiner died in the spring of the following year at age 75. He left a legacy of both triumph and tragedy. Through his many recordings made with the CSO for RCA Victor, he left many memorable recordings. Had he not suffered from such severe personality disorders, there may have been many more. Under Reiner, we also made a series of groundbreaking televised concerts that are still being distributed today. Many of his recordings are considered landmarks, standards by which others are now judged.

As important as the end of the Reiner era was, it was even surpassed by the political moves being made during that year. Those of us in the leadership of the movement that dared to challenge James C. Petrillo's leadership of the Chicago Federation of Musicians decided that there would never be any real reform in the way the union did business unless Petrillo himself was overthrown.

Within just a few years from the time we dared to refuse to apologize to Reiner, our movement began to grow and continue to take on issues that had previously been taken for granted. The long-standing status quo was beginning to crumble. There is a well-known bit of advice that Daniel Burnham, one of Chicago's pioneers had given which we were following. "Make no small plans!"

First, we asked for permission to form an orchestra committee. Then, we proceeded to gain the right of contract ratification. Then, we denied Petrillo a pension. Now, we were bold enough to dream of a musicians union without Jimmy Petrillo. There were many that thought our plans were far too ambitious and unattainable. After all, Petrillo was reputed to be one of the most powerful labor leaders in the history of the United States. But, in a relatively short period of time, we had become a group of somewhat sophisticated political operatives.

As it turned out, we were not yet sophisticated enough to avoid the mistakes that were eventually made.

A political faction within the musicians union, opposed to the current administration, had not existed for more years than anyone could remember. It was obvious right from the beginning that we needed a coalition of musicians from all facets of the music business if we were to succeed. We also needed a simple and understandable goal. The name we adopted for our new faction said it all: Chicago Musicians for Union Democracy (CMUD).

As he had done before, Marvin Rochetti, the free lance musician who played Violin and doubled on Trumpet, joined forces with those of us in the Chicago Symphony who led this movement.

There was a whole agenda of ideas we wanted to bring to the musicians union to reform this antiquated labor organization and bring it, perhaps kicking and screaming, into the twentieth century. Perhaps, it was the times, but we all strongly felt that having segregated Jim Crow musicians' locals in Chicago was no longer acceptable. We believed that every professional musician working in Chicago, regardless of his race, should belong to the same Local and have the same rights.

As we had always done in the past, we sought advice from those whose opinions we valued. Rochetti and I made an appointment with U.S. District Court Judge James B. Parsons, the first black judge to be appointed to the federal bench in Chicago.

He graciously met us in his chambers in the Federal Building. We told him of our plans to integrate the Chicago Federation of Musicians if we could defeat Petrillo's administration in the election that was to be held on December 2, 1962. We asked him for his advice on how we should proceed to merge the two segregated Locals into one integrated union. We believed Parsons would be sympathetic not only because of his race, but because we knew of his musical background during his school days as well.

Instead of giving us the advice we had sought, he spent the next two hours apologizing for, and attempting to explain, what he apparently viewed as the stereotypical behavior of black people. Rochetti and I were not only shocked; we were deeply dismayed and saddened. Apparently, this brilliant jurist had risen to the federal bench by being a professional Uncle Tom. He certainly had no need to grovel before us, but that was exactly what he did. If he behaved that way with us, one can only imagine how he behaved before people with real power. It was a meeting that neither Rochetti nor I will ever forget.

The upcoming election of officers for the Chicago Federation of Musicians, Local 10, AFM, was the first scheduled election mandated by the Labor-Management Reporting and Disclosure Act of 1959 in our Local. Petrillo had gone virtually unchallenged for forty years. There was an occasion years earlier in Local 10's history when Petrillo was challenged. Petrillo simply called the challenger, one Angelo Cavallo, into his office and asked for his union membership card. As soon as it was handed over, Petrillo took it and simply tore it up and kicked the challenger out of the union. The ballots that year read: For President, Vote for One. Of course, there was only one name on the ballot for President, that was James C. Petrillo. In that respect, elections in Local 10 were not very much different than the elections that were held in another union; the Soviet Union.

Chicago Musicians for Union Democracy intended to field an entire slate of candidates in the forthcoming election. We all believed that our first effort would not be entirely victorious. We hoped to gain at least a few offices so that Petrillo would no longer have control of the entire union administration. There were some twenty-two different spots on the ballot. Those included every office from President down to the Sergeant at Arms.

I was chosen to edit and publish our organization's newsletter, which was called *Take Ten*. Those words have a special meaning to musicians and have a double interpretation. "Take ten" is what a bandleader would call out to his musicians when declaring an intermission or break in the rehearsal or performance. But it was also intended to mean, "to take Local 10 away from its current leaders." Everyone in the union understood the significance of our newsletter's name.

With the monthly newsletter being mailed to the entire union membership, we were making great strides in convincing our union's membership that there was a need to "make a clean sweep" at this election. Donations to our cause started to roll into our treasury in unprecedented numbers. We were buoyed beyond imagination.

The really tough decision was to choose the right candidate for each position on the ballot. Because we knew that it was essential to any chance for a victory, some members of the Chicago Symphony offered to run for office. In the case of the full-time positions, it meant giving up your position in the CSO if you were actually elected. But, we were prepared to make that sacrifice in the cause of gaining control of the Local.

Rudy Nashan, one of the Symphony's Trumpet players, offered and was chosen to run for Vice President. I offered and was chosen to run for Recording Secretary. Other CSO members ran for positions on the Board of Directors and the Examining Committee. We eventually chose members of CMUD to run for every position on the ballot.

The most difficult position to fill, obviously, was the candidate for President, as that person would be directly challenging Jimmy Petrillo. In the end, we chose a veteran bandleader named Bernard F. (Barney) Richards as our standard bearer. We knew that as a businessman, he would have the ability to make the necessary executive decisions. Richards actually orchestrated a campaign to win our nomination.

Not only did Richards personally donate a great deal of money to our campaign, he also brought in an old-time lawyer experienced in the rough and tumble of union politics, Francis Heisler, to advise us.

Over the course of the summer and autumn of 1962, CMUD gained a momentum that seemed unstoppable as we gained more and more supporters. As time went on, we actually began to fantasize winning this historic election.

The CMUD Steering Committee, which included Wayne Barrington, a CSO French Horn player, Rudy Nashan, CSO Trumpeter, Bob Clair, free lance Drummer and Teacher, Marvin Rochetti, free lance Violinist and Trumpeter and me, held its periodic meetings in a North Side Chicago bar. It was chosen as a secret out of the way location in which we could gather with complete privacy and security. Never the less, I can still remember several of our members peering out the door to see if the coast was clear before deciding to depart. There was always the fear that some union or Mafia goons would show up one day and beat the Hell out of us to discourage our activities. Fortunately, that never happened.

The union's nominating meeting took place in October. All of the candidates on our slate were nominated without incident. An historic confrontation was in the offing. The union duly printed sample ballots and mailed them to every member of Local 10 along with an official notification of the date, place and time of the election.

When December 2, 1962 actually arrived, we were all anxious about the weather. A nasty or bitterly cold winter day would limit the number of members that would show up to vote. However, the day was relatively mild for Chicago at that time of year. During most of the day, the temperature hovered around the freezing point. There was intermittent light sleet so that the ground was covered with a thin layer of slush. It could have been much worse.

All day long, musicians streamed into and out of the union's headquarters where their votes were cast on a paper ballot in a voting booth. The union's meeting room was a bedlam of activity. Paul Grant, a Professor of Industrial Relations at Loyola University, was selected by mutual consent to take charge of the election. He engaged a number of his students to act as election officials.

When the voting hours finally came to an end, many of the candidates and observers were present as the counters began their task of actually tallying the ballots cast in order to declare the winners. The print and broadcasting news media were there as well. Everyone present knew that regardless of the results, this had been an historic election unmarred by any violence. For that, we were all grateful.

Chicago Symphony percussion section performing in Milwaukee, Wisconsin. Back row, L to R, Sam Denov, Harry Brabec, Gordon Peters and James Gordon (Extra). Next to back row, Al Payson and James Lane, circa 1970.

Sam Denov, age 15, playing Timpani at Lane Tech. H.S., 1939.

Sam Denov playing Timpani at Birch Creek Music Camp, Egg Harbor, Wisconsin, 1992.

Henry Fogel, President, The Orchestral Assn., Sam Denov and Sir Georg Solti following Retirement Ceremony on October 5, 1985.

Autographed photo of Georg Solti to Sam Denov, 1970.

Sam Denov and Al Payson rehearsing their parts for *Echoes of Time and the River*, by George Crumm.

Fritz Reiner studying score at his estate in Westport, Connecticut, circa 1955.

Carlotta and Fritz Reiner smiling at estate in Westport, Connecticut, circa 1955.

Believed to be the last photo taken of Sir Georg Solti by Lady Valerie Solti.

Francis Akos, Violin, Sam Denov and Victor Aitay, Violin, shown with Jack Benny in his suite at the Ambassador East Hotel, Chicago, 1962.

Percussion and Timpani sections of Chicago Symphony on tour, 1965. Shown L to R, Al Payson, James J. Ross, Gordon Peters, Donald Koss, Sam Denov and Harry Brabec.

Recording at Sofiensaal, Vienna, Austria, 1971.

Dave Greenbaum, 'Cello, being greeted by Bagpipe Band in Glasgow, Scotland, 1971.

Publicity shot of Percussion and Timpani sections for Japanese tour, 1977.
Shown L to R, James Lane, Sam Denov, Al Payson, Gordon Peters and Donald
Koss.

Sam Denov and Donald Koss shown rehearsing at Orchestra Hall, Chicago, 1975.

Chapter 8

The Election Results

Because the greatest interest was in the outcome of the election for President of the Local, all the unfolded marked ballots were taken out of the locked ballot box and initially separated into two stacks, those marked for Petrillo and those marked for Richards. The vast majority of the ballots were straight ticket votes, either for or against the Petrillo slate. It was rare indeed to come across a ballot that was marked for some of the Petrillo candidates and also some of the CMUD candidates.

There was a great deal of commotion in the meeting hall and it was absolutely impossible to say with any degree of certainty that all the individuals there were those who were authorized to be there. There was a perception that security within the hall was not as tight as it should have been. Outside the meeting hall, hundreds of people were milling about waiting for the results to be announced. Suddenly, the doors were opened and those waiting outside the meeting room were allowed inside.

After many hours of mindless speculation, Paul Grant stepped onto the dais and was prepared to announce the winning candidates for each office. I was waiting for the results with mixed emotions because if the CMUD slate was as successful as we had hoped, it would mean that I would have to resign from the Chicago Symphony in order to be sworn into office as the new Recording Secretary of Local 10 in January, 1963.

A hush fell over all those present as Grant began to read the final results. He announced, "I'm going to read the final results of the tally and mention only the names of the winning candidates without announcing the final vote tallies. It will take several days before all the absentee ballots have been counted. It's anticipated, however, that the final results will not change substantially from what I'm about to announce tonight. Therefore, what I'll be announcing will be only the results of the balloting that took place in this room today. I hope that everyone here understands that the final results may change somewhat, but not decisively."

"In the contest for President of Local 10, the winning candidate is Bernard F. (Barney) Richards!" The hall erupted into a deafening roar as members of CMUD looked at each other incredulously. We had actually defeated one of the most powerful labor leaders in the United States. We couldn't believe what we were hearing. Grant appealed for order so that he could continue reading the rest of the results.

After some time, he continued to read the rest of the results. "For Vice President, Rudolph Nashan." Again, there was considerable commotion because the losing Vice President had been Carl A. Baumann, a long-time associate of Petrillo. After order was again established, Grant continued. For Treasurer, Ervin I. Trisko." So far, CMUD was making a clean sweep of the election. The losing candidate for Treasurer had been an incumbent, one of Petrillo's sons.

Grant continued, "For Recording Secretary, Leo H. Nye." I stood there not believing what I was hearing, dumbfounded! I asked myself how this could have happened? Had the members really rejected my candidacy? I felt betrayed and yet very excited that our slate appeared to be winning until now.

As Grant continued to read off the names of the winning candidates, all of our CMUD candidates were named winners except Raymond Sergo and me. Sergo had been one of our candidates for the Board of Directors. The only winners among the Petrillo candidates had been Nye, who defeated me to be reelected Recording Secretary, and Dan Garamoni who defeated Ray Sergo for a seat on the Board of Directors. Both Nye and Garamoni were Petrillo stalwarts. There was something about these results that seemed incongruous to me. Despite my personal loss, CMUD members were overcome with joy.

Our political faction had made history and this stunning upset was reported in the media from coast to coast. We had put Petrillo out to pasture, so to speak, so we had much to celebrate regardless of my loss and that of Ray Sergo. Considering that we only hoped to make some inroads and build for the future, CMUD had been imminently successful.

I was not overjoyed by my defeat, although I had been spared the agony of giving up my career as a member of the Chicago Symphony. At the time, I was mourning my loss with my wife and two young sons, all of who were overjoyed at the prospect that I would continue my lifelong career goal as a CSO member. To them, my defeat was a blessing in disguise. They had never supported the idea that I might change my career path from musician to union politician.

Although I participated in all the revelry that took place in our CMUD camp, I did so with a heavy heart. Everyone was too busy enjoying this sweet victory to even consider how I felt about my defeat. I had devoted so much to this cause and would now have nothing personal to show for it.

In the days that followed our victory, I spent a great deal of time with Barney Richards, briefing him on all the problems in the Chicago Symphony that needed to be addressed by his new administration.

He was very sympathetic and seemed to fully understand the complexities of the problems in the Symphony even though his experience had been mainly as a danceband leader. During all this time, Bob Clair and I had also been very close. Perhaps because he was a fellow Percussionist, although a free lancer, we struck a mutual chord in our relationship. He seemed to feel the pain and anguish that I was feeling. It was a very heavy emotional burden to carry when I thought about the many that had rejected my bid to become the Local 10 Recording Secretary. I even thought that perhaps I had become too familiar to the union's members because of my many writings in CMUD's *Take Ten*. I had temporarily forgotten about all those that had voted for me because of my preoccupation with those that had voted against me and for Leo Nye.

But, the election was over and Jimmy Petrillo was part of the history of Local 10 now. Although I attended the inauguration ceremonies for the new administration in January, I took no special joy in it. Even the appearance of George Jessel as Master of Ceremonies did not lift the gloom that I felt. It was difficult not to focus on the negatives that life had dealt me. Although I continued as Chairman of the CSO Members' Committee and as Vice Chairman of ICSOM, I had a feeling of melancholia that I simply could not get beyond. There was just something about the results of this election that stuck in my craw and didn't make any sense to me. The question that was nagging at my conscience was just how did this happen, and why did it happen to me?

I initiated my own investigation of the conduct of this election. If there was something unlawful that had happened to deny me the victory I felt I should have had, I simply wanted to know what it was. Perhaps I would even regain what had been denied. I began to study the requirements of the new Labor Management Reporting and Disclosure Act of 1959 regarding the conduct and challenge of local union elections. There was something fishy about this election, but I still didn't know what it was.

News that I was considering a challenge of the conduct of the election was beginning to become known among those members who were concerned about such matters. No one wanted to overturn the results of the election in a way that would deny Richards the Presidency. It was about that time that I began receiving the first of many mysterious phone calls from someone who claimed to be a Local 10 member that I had never met. He told me things that I had a very hard time swallowing. He said that he had some vague connections with "the boys" whom I understood to be members of the Mafia or some organized crime family.

He said that "the boys" were rather unhappy about the way the election had turned out. At first, I wasn't quite sure just what he was talking about. In time, and after receiving several of these mysterious phone calls, I finally began to understand just what he was getting at. He always spoke in rather vague terms. It turned out that "the boys" wanted to make sure that whatever happened in this election, Petrillo would remain in power. But apparently, those who had been charged with that responsibility had bungled the job. Because "the boys" were miffed, my caller was going to supply me with information that could assure my challenge would have substance. The strange part was that there was nothing particular that was wanted from me in exchange for this information. I had no reason whatever to doubt the veracity of what I was being told.

From the bits and pieces of information I received, I put together the following scenario. It was Nye and Garamoni who had been charged with the responsibility of seeing to Petrillo's reelection. As a former Field Officer for the National Labor Relations Board, Nye had conducted many representation elections and knew all the ins and outs of how elections were conducted. As the Local's Recording Secretary, he had the responsibility of printing the paper ballots and verifying the authenticity of the ballots cast. No one, it seems, had any knowledge of just how many election ballots had actually been printed and whether they had all been accounted for. Garamoni was involved only because he had been chosen as the heir apparent to succeed Petrillo when the time came. So, it became important that these two also remained in office at Local 10.

What had happened was that when the ballots were segregated into two stacks at the counting table following the close of the balloting, one stack of which were Petrillo ballots and the other larger stack for Richards, approximately 300 ballots marked for Richards had been stolen. They were removed unnoticed from the room in all the noise and confusion. They were replaced with 300 phony ballots marked for Petrillo, Nye and Garamoni that had apparently been supplied by Nye. It had been anticipated that the additional 300 ballots for these three and the 300 fewer votes for Richards would be sufficient to assure the desired outcome of the election. But there was a miscalculation.

The shift in the numbers was sufficient to assure the election of Nye and Garamoni, but was insufficient to defeat Richards. They had underestimated the number of ballots that had been cast for Richards. The theft of the ballots, I was told, was accomplished by Nick Acerenza, the long-time janitor for the union building. I was also informed that the stolen ballots were still in his possession.

With this hearsay evidence, I filed a challenge of the election with the U.S. Labor Department, alleging all the irregularities that I knew had taken place. During the investigation of the election, which took a number of months, I was informed by the investigating agent that the stolen ballots had been anonymously mailed to the Labor Department. To the best of my knowledge, those ballots are still in the files of the Labor Department in Chicago.

But my efforts to set the election right ultimately failed. I eventually received word from the Labor Department that my challenge was denied. They concluded that although all the irregularities I had alleged had actually taken place, they did not affect the outcome of the election. Their logic entirely escaped me, but I was powerless to challenge their decision. I felt that the Labor Department's decision was strictly a political one made by the then Secretary of Labor, Arthur Goldberg. The decision had no relationship to the facts. But that decision was not appealable. The case was closed, and as a result, I remained a member of the Chicago Symphony Orchestra.

Chapter 9

The Trusteeship

The new administration of Local 10 took office amid great expectations. One of its first acts was to initiate the proceedings to merge the Chicago Musicians Club with the union. The Chicago Musicians Club owned the building that housed the union's headquarters on West Washington Street. This had been a tactical move by Petrillo to shield the headquarters building in the event there was ever a judgment against the union. Every member of the union also held membership in the Club. There was no telling how much money had been siphoned off the union's treasury and transferred into the treasury of the Club.

In these efforts, Richards' attorney, Francis Heisler, assisted by Chicago attorney Marc Schwartz, handled the legal papers. The next order of business was to begin negotiations with the officers of Local 208, AFM, to merge the segregated unions. Because the officers of Local 208 feared they would be somehow shuffled out of their leadership posts, these negotiations became difficult and lengthy.

During these first few months of the new administration, things dramatically improved for the Chicago Symphony. The new Board of Directors of Local 10 adopted a new set of Rules and Regulations for the new Union Steward of the CSO. These were drafted by me and were adopted precisely as I had written them. They are still in operation today, included by reference in every succeeding contract the union has negotiated with The Orchestral Association.

Richards had begun to put a new staff together of his own choices to assist him in operating the union. Little by little, the people he had trusted as members of CMUD were being replaced. It soon became apparent that the AFM was making great efforts to slow the new administration down in its reforms of the union. Apparently, Richards was being compromised by the AFM.

During the AFM convention of June 1963, Petrillo was invited to address the delegates as a guest speaker. At the time, he had no official title of any kind within the structure of the AFM. During a lengthy speech at the convention, which was recorded and sent to all the Locals in the Federation, Petrillo cursed out those who had defeated him and forced him out of office as President of Local 10. We were referred to as "traitors" and worse by Petrillo.

Local 10 was duly informed by the IEB that negotiations to merge the segregated Locals in Chicago were moving ahead too slowly. The International Executive Board of the AFM named Petrillo as the new Chairman of its Civil Rights Department. This was really ironic because, over the years, Petrillo had been the principal impediment to the merger of Local 10 with Local 208. Many times over the years, the officers of Local 208 had requested that their Local be merged with Local 10. It had always been Petrillo who had denied those requests. This was simply an excuse to provide Petrillo with a job and a salary.

Suddenly, like a bolt of lightning out of the blue, Local 10 was informed by the AFM that it was being placed in trusteeship. The AFM was using its legal powers to take over the Local and its treasury, naming Hal C. Davis, President of the Pittsburgh Local and a member of the IEB, to act as the Trustee, with complete authority to run the Local.

Suddenly, Davis, rather than Richards, was running our Local. Although none of us had ever met Davis previously, we recognized him as one of those who were in attendance at the meeting of Local 10 when we had denied Petrillo a pension. Suddenly, it seemed that everything we had worked for was in jeopardy. Had the AFM outfoxed us? Had everything we had accomplished been for nothing?

Officially, Local 10 had been placed in trusteeship in order to accomplish the merger of Local 208 with Local 10, which had been mandated by the new Civil Rights laws. The merger, however, would have taken place regardless of the intrusion of the AFM. It was simply being used as a pretext to take back control of Local 10 from this group of "insurgents" and "traitors." Every reform that had been planned for Local 10 was put on hold. We were in a state of suspended animation.

However, a significant change did take place. Richards' attorneys, Heisler and Schwartz, were replaced by the law firm of Asher, Greenfield and Gubbins, a Chicago labor law firm that represented a number of AFL-CIO unions. It was obviously this new law firm's job to see that nothing was ever undertaken by Local 10-208 from that day on that was not approved by the AFM. That law firm continues to represent the Local to this very day.

Fortunately for the CSO Members' Committee, Davis did not lift a finger to interfere with anything that was going on within the Chicago Symphony. My own assessment of the situation was that Davis was fearful of tangling with the members of the Chicago Symphony. It was well known that the defeat of Petrillo would never have happened without the leadership of the Symphony musicians in Local 10.

While my duties as Vice Chairman of ICSOM did not consume very much of my time or efforts in those days, I continued to communicate with George Zazofsky to keep him informed of what was happening in Chicago. He was very much dismayed by the events that had taken place. He knew full well that the AFM had used one of its ultimate control weapons to assure its supremacy of the musicians' union. Apparently, though Kenin had appeared cooperative, he was capable of using the union's muscle when he believed the conditions warranted it. This use of muscle in Chicago did not augur well for ICSOM's future relationship with the AFM.

ICSOM continued to forge ahead, doing things that the union should have been doing, but never did. Bob Coleman, the CSO Violist who had been active in CMUD, edited ICSOM's journal, aptly named Senza Sordino (Without Mute) by Joane Bennett, a CSO Flautist. His unique writing capabilities and humor made the journal an absolute delight to read. Unfortunately, Coleman resigned from the Chicago Symphony in 1964 to accept a teaching position at the University of Connecticut at Storrs, where he also became a resident member of the university's string quartet. Coleman's departure from Chicago was a great loss to all of us.

Our season of guest conductors after Reiner's departure from the CSO yielded a number of candidates eager to take over the Orchestra's helm. The Orchestral Association's Trustees ultimately selected Jean Martinon as the new Music Director of the CSO. He had made a very strong impression during his guest conducting stint with the CSO, and was eagerly anticipated as the new Maestro beginning with the 1963-64 season.

He was most anxious to be accepted by the musicians of the Orchestra as their new leader. When he arrived in Chicago a few days before the beginning of his first season, he took the trouble to arrange personal meetings with the Members' Committee at his apartment to get acquainted. However, the French maestro took great pains to insure that our meetings were not known by the CSO's Trustees. This was certainly a radical departure from our relationship with Reiner.

Unbeknown to our Percussion section, Edward Metzenger, our Timpanist, retired at the end of the 1963 Ravinia season after 31 years as a member of the CSO. Neither he nor anyone else ever mentioned a word about it until Martinon's first season began. Reiner had never succeeded in replacing him.

With the opening of the Martinon era came the appearance of our new Timpanist, Donald A. Koss. The retirement of Metzenger and the engagement of Koss were a complete mystery to those of us in the Percussion section. Koss's only professional experience was a single season with the Grant Park Symphony Orchestra. He was a self-taught musician who gave up a career as a Math teacher at Evanston Township High School to join the orchestra. Martinon had never auditioned him before he was engaged, so far as we knew. There were still things going on at Orchestra Hall that were a complete enigma to the musicians of the CSO.

61

Chapter 10

Martinon

As a new era began in the autumn of 1963 with Jean Martinon at the helm of the Chicago Symphony Orchestra, it was inevitable that changes were about to take place. Of course, Martinon was very pleased with the caliber of the orchestra he inherited from Fritz Reiner. A full season of guest conductors had not dimmed any of its luster.

From a physical standpoint, Martinon was the antithesis of Fritz Reiner. While not a tall man, he appeared to be very physically fit. He stood very erect, was very trim, and sported a closely cropped head of gunmetal gray hair. If one didn't know what his vocation was, he could easily be mistaken for a U.S. Marine Corps Drill Sergeant. Somehow, he never looked totally relaxed.

Rather than using the vest-pocket style of conducting Reiner had been noted for, our new French Music Director conducted in a no-nonsense clean manner that even the most inexperienced musician would have no trouble following. The start of his tenure with the CSO was notable for the increased amount of French music being programmed for the Orchestra.

Reiner had been a master of many different styles of music while Martinon's repertoire seemed to be rooted in Western and Central European music. It was difficult not to make comparisons during the first few years of Martinon's tenure. While Reiner's concerts could be very exciting, Martinon's seemed to have less spontaneity and more routine. His concerts were always well crafted, but only rarely exciting. Whatever composition he conducted, he could always be relied upon to do it in exactly the same manner the next time it was performed.

Rehearsals with Martinon were almost always quite pleasant and relaxed. Few of us saw any further need to always be on the edge of our seat. During his first few years, he was very friendly and open with the members of the Orchestra. But as time wore on, and his concerts did not always receive the rave reviews he would have liked, he gradually began to loose some of the self-assurance he had started with. We began to do more domestic touring and his concerts were always well received. A highlight of his tenure was a tour to the West Coast, the Pacific Northwest, Vancouver, Anchorage, Fairbanks and Winnipeg. We did do some recording, but The Orchestral Association subsidized many of these.

As mentioned previously, the fact that the union was in trusteeship had relatively little impact on our lives in the Chicago Symphony. We continued to institute small improvements in our working conditions that eventually had the cumulative effect of a more comfortable and pleasant working environment. We were the first Symphony in the country to include a contractual clause that said we could not be required to perform for a segregated audience. Even Dr. Oldberg was beginning to accept the notion that the Members' Committee was going to have a continuing presence on the CSO and the relationship between its employees and their employer.

At the union, the negotiations to merge Chicago's two musicians' Locals continued unabated. In time, a formula was worked out where a number of positions on the union's administration were guaranteed to the former members of Local 208 for a number of years. When the guarantee would expire some years in the future, there would be a return to normalcy with anyone eligible to hold any office he or she was elected to. The merged union became known as the Chicago Federation of Musicians, Local 10-208, AFM. The offices and property of the former Local 208 were disposed of in accordance with the agreement reached between the Locals. The merged Local's membership now stood at approximately 16,000.

It was during Martinon's tenure that Orchestra Hall began having structural problems, which created a number of challenges for the CSO management. In addition, Seymour Raven, the troublesome manager of the CSO who came on board during Reiner's final years, was persuaded to retire and take on a position arranged for him by Dr. Oldberg. He became the Director of Organizations and Activities for the Chicago Circle Campus of the University of Illinois. We laughingly referred to his new position as the "DOA of Circle Campus." In America's hospital emergency rooms, "DOA" means "dead on arrival."

Replacing Seymour Raven was John Edwards, the highly regarded Manager of the Pittsburgh Symphony Orchestra. With Edwards, we finally found the Manager we could do business with. He was very savvy about this business and had the ability to work with orchestra committees as the expected means by which relationships with employees were normally handled. While Edwards and the Members' Committee each represented their respective constituencies with zeal, much of the acrimony disappeared from our relationship.

It was not until many years later, after Edwards had passed on and I had retired from the Orchestra, that I learned from his longtime Secretary, Teresa Amling, that whenever he knew that there was a meeting coming up at which I would be present, he would start quaking and becoming extremely nervous and agitated. Apparently, he feared having to deal with me. He certainly did an excellent job of hiding those feelings when he was in my presence. Obviously, he was the consummate professional.

During the middle 1960's, the old Pullman Standard Building, a brownstone gem that stood directly north of Orchestra Hall on Michigan Avenue, was demolished to make room for the erection of the Borg-Warner Building. Once the old building was gone, with nothing there other than a very large hole in the earth, Orchestra Hall, erected in 1905 on wooden pilings in sand, began to slowly tilt to the north. A crevice gradually started opening up between Orchestra Hall and the building to its south, the Railroad Exchange Building.

While rehearsing at Orchestra Hall, one could occasionally hear cracking noises and view small bits of plaster falling from the proscenium onto the stage. It was not long before Orchestra Hall was declared temporarily unsafe and all of our operations had to be moved to the Medinah Temple. The Temple was an old Shriner's auditorium on the Near North Side of the city with very sonorous acoustics. Orchestra Hall was eventually shored up and we were permitted to move back there.

With all of this architectural work going on around us, it was deemed an appropriate time to schedule some needed renovations for Orchestra Hall. To install a new heating and air conditioning system in the auditorium, the architects chose to change the solid plaster proscenium over the stage into a perforated surface through which air could flow. The architects assured The Orchestral Association that the change would not adversely affect the acoustics of Orchestra Hall, but if it did, they would be able to restore the old acoustics. While the stage had always had some problems for the musicians hearing each other, the old hall was a superb recording studio.

Assurances notwithstanding, the change in the stage's proscenium had a disastrous effect acoustically. Try as they might, all efforts to restore the original acoustics were a failure. The Hall became a very dry acoustical chamber, which made the Orchestra's sound seem hard and brittle. Reverberation time was reduced still further when an audience was present. Acousticians were brought in to work on the problem and there were incremental improvements in time. But sadly, the original acoustics of Orchestra Hall were lost forever.

During this period, our new Timpanist, Donald Koss, continued to have his share of problems. For some reason, the Chicago music critics were not very impressed with Koss' playing. One critic even claimed that he became lost during a performance of Stravinsky's *Rite of Spring*. That simply was not true. But this badgering by the press did have its effect on Koss's self image. He became very insecure and sought out the friendship of everyone and anyone in the Orchestra he believed could do him some good.

He made a particularly persistent effort to secure my friendship. And for some time during his early years in the Orchestra, we were very close friends. However, there was always something about his personality that didn't seem genuine. For a long time, I simply couldn't define what it was about him that was flawed, but I was convinced that there was something.

He was an intelligent and well-educated individual with an uncanny sense of recall. After playing a round of golf with him, for instance, he could recount every shot he had made during the entire round with a degree of accuracy that astounded me. He used that unique ability in his musical performances. Once he had played a particular composition, even one he had never performed before, he never made a mistake in a subsequent replaying and could always be relied upon to perform his part accurately. While there were some that did not like the sound he produced any more than they liked Metzenger's, he managed to hang on and become accepted as the Orchestra's Timpanist.

James J. Ross did not fare as well. Before Reiner concluded his tenure with the CSO, he attempted to discharge Ross after finally becoming disenchanted with his performing ability. Reiner was certainly not known for his loyalty. At one point, Reiner told him, "I would call you a shoemaker, but I wouldn't want to insult their profession."

Ross had made many sacrifices over the years for Reiner. Since beginning to work for him back in 1927, he had moved himself and his family to several different cities when Reiner beckoned him and asked for his help. Now that he was getting older and his skills were not quite as sharp as they had once been, Reiner was ready to abandon him.

Ross appealed to the Members' Committee for help. On that occasion, we were able to intervene with Dr. Oldberg and save his job. But now, a few years later, Ross' playing was again becoming a problem in the Percussion section. This was Martinon's regime now and not Reiner's. In addition, Gordon Peters, our new Principal, simply didn't like the way Ross played. Ross was finally persuaded to voluntarily resign. He wanted to continue performing, however, despite his age. He was able to secure a position with the Alabama Symphony in Birmingham, and continued playing there until he eventually died of a heart attack some years later.

Harry Brabec, my old friend and the Principal Percussionist that Reiner had let go, returned to the roster as a Librarian during Martinon's tenure. After a few years, he was advanced to the post of Stage Manager. He was always available to play extra Percussion with us and was utilized often.

However, by 1971, he asked for a raise in salary and told John Edwards that if it was not forthcoming, he would resign his position. Again, Brabec had taken a calculated risk as he had often done with Reiner, but this time, his bluff was called and he carried out his threat to resign.

Chapter 11

The Aftermath

After several seasons had passed with Martinon, and he had become less secure, he began a period of withdrawal. He spent more time then ever locked away in his dressing room, communicating only with trusted allies in the Orchestra.

His insecurity was also reflected in his music making. An able and experienced conductor knows intuitively when to tighten the controls and when to loosen them so that the Orchestra can play by itself at times, without too much "interference" from its director. Martinon's conducting became more and more controlled over time. When controls are never relaxed, an orchestra can feel too tightly controlled, and the music reflects these feelings in its performances. The zest, spontaneity and pleasure of the music seem to disappear. It simply wasn't as comfortable playing with Martinon as it had been.

Gradually, the Orchestra, which had accepted him with open arms, was beginning to pull back. His concerts were becoming more like hard work rather than a joyous experience.

The reviews of Martinon's concerts were not as favorable as they had been. The musicians were beginning to feel like victims again. The future prospects with Martinon, which had looked so bright when he first arrived, were beginning to fade. The Orchestra's perception of his value also started to fade. Even the audiences were withdrawing their loyalty to him. Concert attendance began to drop off. By the end of Martinon's fourth season, it became apparent that The Orchestral Association would soon have to look for a replacement for Martinon.

James J. Ross had now been replaced by James Lane, a graduate of Ball State University in Muncie, Indiana. Lane was chosen by an unbiased audition system we had put in place some years before. Gone were the days when a recommendation by the right person was good enough to get you into the CSO. Lane was an excellent Percussionist who fit in with our Percussion section like a custom made glove. It seemed that every time a Percussionist left the CSO, he was replaced by a congenial and highly skilled performer, for which we were very grateful.

As the merged union finally began to operate as an entity, the reins of the AFM's trusteeship began to slacken and were finally removed. By then, Richards had been so discredited as a leader that there wasn't even a hint that he would run for reelection in December of 1965. And he didn't.

In that election of officers, the first for the newly merged Local, Dan Garamoni, who had been serving on the Board of Directors and was Petrillo's heir apparent, made his bid for the leadership of the Local. Rudy Nashan, the Vice President, also thought it was time to run for President. During the three years he had served as Vice President, he somehow seemed to have lost his direction and the ideals for which he had offered to give up his position in the CSO. It seemed that now, he was simply another politician who was willing to do just about anything to keep feeding at the trough. The notion of Petrillo attempting to make a comeback was simply out of the question.

Having gone through the investigation of its last election and the means by which it was conducted, Local 10-208 decided that this time, there would be no paper ballots used. Mechanical voting machines were rented from the Cook County Board of Election Commissioners and used in the union's election for the very first time. Paul Grant was again selected to take charge of the election. This time there was more confidence that the announced results at the conclusion of the voting would be accurate and could be relied upon. To virtually no one's surprise, Dan Garamoni was declared the winner and new President of Local 10-208.

Crestfallen, Nashan and his family left Chicago and secured a position with the Syracuse Symphony Orchestra in New York State as the orchestra's Personnel Manager and Utility Trumpet.

None of the CSO members, other than Violinist Joseph Golan, chose to remain on the union's roster of officers. Golan was handily reelected to the Board of Directors where he served a second and final term while continuing to play with the Symphony.

Year after year, I was reelected to the Members' Committee where I served as Chairman and as Union Steward for a good number of years. I also continued as Vice Chairman of ICSOM, the players' conference, while George Zazofsky of the Boston Symphony continued as Chairman.

While ICSOM's relationship with the AFM was still somewhat strained, the AFM did begin to make small concessions. AFM President Herman Kenin began to relax and his fears that ICSOM would bolt the union began to fade. He designated one of his Presidential Assistants as head of Symphony affairs on a part-time basis. Of course, he didn't do nearly enough to satisfy the needs symphony musicians had nor deliver the services that were expected.

Zazofsky and I met more frequently with Kenin in New York, and the tension between us began to relax. Of course, things may have been different if we had been using more pressure on Kenin to do the many things symphony musicians wanted from their union. But, there was a feeling that in time, the AFM would be more forthcoming and begin treating symphony musicians with some respect.

Various talented musicians took turns editing ICSOM's journal, *Senza Sordino*, which finally settled on a format in which the pages were printed on 8½ x 11 pages, small enough to be read on a music stand during rehearsals when one was not busy playing. *Senza Sordino* was beginning to regularly carry a wealth of useful material on its pages, including comprehensive charts of comparative wage scales, working conditions and other pertinent information.

Pressure was building for the financing of a special strike fund for symphony and opera musicians whom had never had one. Since most of the member orchestras in ICSOM did not have year-round seasons, musicians could ill afford to go on strike for better wages and working conditions.

When ICSOM had first formalized its organization, there were many who suspected that this was a subversive organization that was somehow planning to take over America's symphony orchestras. Walter Trohan, a syndicated writer on labor matters for the *Chicago Tribune* wrote about his suspicions of ICSOM's motives. He said that the organization was headed by two musicians with Russian names (Zazofsky and Denov) and published a newsletter with a strange Italian name (*Senza Sordino*).

He believed that the organization needed to be watched even though a FBI search of the leaders' Communist records turned up nothing. The article was really laughable but indicated how suspicious and paranoid some of America's wealthy arts patrons were. What is really remarkable is that these same arts patrons had no fears whatsoever of the AFM and its representation of these musicians.

In the late 1960's, Dr. Eric Oldberg finally retired from his medical and teaching careers. He also retired as Chairman of The Orchestral Association's Board of Trustees. The Trustees, possibly weary of Oldberg's authoritarian style of leadership, elected Louis C. Sudler, a real estate tycoon, as its new Chairman. A tall, handsome man with chiseled features, who had once had ambitions of becoming a professional opera baritone, was an entirely new style of leader for the CSO. He actually loved and respected musicians.

One of his first acts was to meet with the leadership of the CSO Members' Committee. We really didn't know what to expect when we were invited to his sumptuous offices in the Hancock Center, one of Chicago's tallest buildings. His real estate firm had been the developers of the Hancock Center.

He greeted us with a warm smile and welcomed us into his office. He got right to the point immediately. He told us that Martinon's unsuccessful tenure as Music Director of the Chicago Symphony was coming to an end. He told us of his visions of making the Chicago Symphony Orchestra known as the world's greatest orchestra. And then he asked us a question that absolutely astounded us.

Now that he had John Edwards on board as the orchestra's excellent manager, he wanted our opinions on which conductors we would recommend to become the next Music Director, someone who was capable of putting our orchestra in the world's spotlight. We were truly speechless. No one had ever valued our professional opinion before. Now, we were being asked whom in the world we believed could lead the CSO to the pinnacle of world fame!

We looked at each other in disbelief for a moment and then came up with a trio of names. Our unanimous first choice, if he was available and willing to come, was Herbert Von Karajan, Music Director of the Berlin Philharmonic. Sudler listened without batting an eye. Then he said, "And who would be your second choice if we're somehow not able to get Von Karajan?"

We thought, *O my God, he's really serious!* We were united in our choice for a fallback Music Director. Our next choice was Carlo Maria Guilini, the brilliant and handsome Italian conductor who had made a huge success in his guest conducting dates with the CSO. We cautioned that Guilini might not be willing to take on the administrative duties of a Music Director. He was known to hate having to deal with the business of running an orchestra. He simply wanted to make beautiful music. And then, Sudler asked us for a third choice, in the event Edwards was unable to secure the services of either of the first two. We simply couldn't believe that a Chairman of the Symphony's Trustees was seriously asking and taking our advice in this manner.

That was when we suggested Georg Solti, Music Director of London's Covent Garden Opera Company. He had guest conducted us during a summer season at Ravinia and had been a huge success with both audience and orchestra.

Sudler said, "Fine, I'll get John Edwards on it right away. I really appreciate your help in coming up here on such short notice." He was thanking us when we should have been groveling at his feet. We still couldn't quite believe what had just taken place.

True to what we had been told, John Edwards did report to us periodically on the results of his quest. In the end, it had been just as we had imagined. Von Karajan was flattered at the offer but respectfully refused, saying his commitments could not possibly allow him to take on the Chicago Symphony.

Guilini, who loved the musicians of the Chicago Symphony, was also flattered at the offer, but turned it down citing his hatred of administrative duties.

Solti was delighted with the offer and accepted it. That was how Solti became the next Music Director of the Chicago Symphony Orchestra, succeeding Jean Martinon in 1969. Perhaps, and this is merely speculation, if he had known that he was the third choice, he may not have accepted the offer. We never revealed how Solti had come to be chosen to anyone. We knew that our historic meeting with Sudler was far too sensitive to ever disclose before now. Most of the principals that were involved are now deceased and I am finally able to share a secret I have kept for all these years.

Chapter 12

Solti Takes Over

Georg Solti, the Hungarian conductor and pianist who spent World War II in Switzerland earning his living as a pianist, became the new Music Director of the Chicago Symphony Orchestra amid much fanfare beginning with the 1969-70 season. As he was beginning his tenure as Music Director of the CSO, I was spending a single year as Chairman of ICSOM.

In 1968, George Zazofsky, the popular Chairman of ICSOM, informed me that he was seriously considering an offer to teach Violin at the University of Miami in Florida. He would be granted a full professorship and be able to play his beloved game of golf every morning of the year. He had grown weary of the Boston Symphony Orchestra and the tribulations of heading an insurgent group such as ICSOM. If he resigned from the Boston Symphony, he realized that he would no longer be qualified to serve as an officer of ICSOM.

In the meanwhile, at the suggestion of Ralph Mendelsohn, a member of the New York Philharmonic-Symphony Orchestra and recent addition to our ICSOM Governing Board, ICSOM engaged a New York attorney by the name of I. Philip Sipser. It was believed that we needed an attorney to steer us through the rocks and shoals of our continuing informal relationship with the AFM. Sipser had represented New York's Brewery Workers before taking on a problem for the New York Philharmonic, which he successfully resolved. I had been the lone holdout in the discussion of whether ICSOM needed a lawyer.

The delegates had instructed the ICSOM Governing Board to seek a charter as a Conference for ICSOM from the AFM. At that point, the AFM had no player conferences. The only conferences were regional ones composed of AFM Locals. I could see no particular advantage in achieving conference status from the AFM. I believed ICSOM would be far better off as an independent conference, but I was unable to convince either the delegates or the Governing Board of the merits of my position.

Against that background, Zazofsky finally decided to accept the full professorship from the University of Miami and resigned his position as a Violinist with the Boston Symphony Orchestra. The ICSOM conference of August 1969 was Zazofsky's last as Chairman. I was elevated to the position of Chairman and Ralph Mendelsohn became the Vice-Chairman.

While I wasn't in total agreement with my colleagues on the ICSOM Governing Board, I forged ahead with the agenda that we had committed ourselves to. Our attorney, Phil Sipser, met frequently with AFM officers and finally convinced them of the merits of granting conference status to ICSOM.

My year as Chairman was a busy one, meeting with AFM officers in New York, trying to put out a fire of a controversy in the San Antonio Symphony over the dismissal of a committee member there, initiating meetings with the Chairperson of the new National Endowment for the Arts, Nancy Hanks, in Washington, all while working on a proposal for a strike fund for symphony and opera musicians.

We were finally successful in persuading Herman Kenin, AFM President, to fund the start-up of a strike fund and he asked me to draft a proposal showing precisely how it would work. In substantive part, Kenin accepted my proposal and I was named one of the fund's initial Trustees.

However, during that year, I often called upon Sipser for assistance, which was not forthcoming. He made himself singularly unavailable to me. I was so upset that by the end of the year, I recommended that we dispense with Sipser's services. My recommendation was not acted upon.

The 1970 ICSOM conference took place in Chicago. Ralph Mendelsohn was not able to attend because he was on tour with the New York Philharmonic. When the time came for the delegates to elect their officers, both Mendelsohn and I were nominated for Chairman. I wasn't too concerned about my election as Chairman and didn't spend any time whatever campaigning for the office.

For the second time in my political life, I lost an election. It was Mendelsohn, and not me, that was elected Chairman of ICSOM. I was more than upset by this surprising turn of events. It was extremely difficult to chair the remainder of the conference that had just rejected my leadership. I'm not sure to what I can attribute my loss, but I highly suspect that somehow, Sipser may have been involved in this debacle. But, it could just as well have been my unwillingness to go along with what I believed were ill-advised strategies.

Regardless of my downfall as Chairman of ICSOM, I continued to be involved in the CSO Members' Committee and participated in the negotiations for every succeeding collective bargaining agreement between The Orchestral Association and Local 10-208.

This man Solti, who conducted with such spastic movements, who came to be known as "The Screaming Skull", took to the CSO like a duck takes to water. That is a cliché, of course, but it accurately describes what happened when he and the CSO joined forces. No one could have anticipated that this coupling of conductor and orchestra would produce what critics later described as "a marriage made in Heaven!"

By the time Solti arrived in Chicago, the CSO had already expanded its season to year-round employment for its musicians. Even the eight weeks that were performed for the Ravinia Festival were now covered in the same single comprehensive collective bargaining agreement. What had been a single typewritten sheet now filled a ½ inch thick booklet printed in a very small typeface.

With Solti now at the helm, expectations were enormous. His subscription weeks sold out so quickly, there was barely a need to advertise them. We began recording for London/Decca Records, with which Solti had enjoyed a long-term relationship. These recordings proved to be so popular that a number of recording companies began lining up for the opportunity to record with the Chicago Symphony. Virtually every well-known conductor who came to Chicago wanted to record with our orchestra.

John Edwards, in his wisdom, did not enter into an exclusive arrangement with any single recording company. That left us free to record with any company willing to pay our fees. There were seasons that we recorded with a number of different companies. In addition to London/Decca, there was Deutsche Grammophon, RCA, Angel and others.

The Solti/Chicago Symphony combination became so popular that we began winning Grammys at an unprecedented rate. During my remaining years with the CSO with Solti as Music Director, we garnered a minimum of two dozen Grammy awards, more than any other orchestra in the history of the awards.

Wisely, Solti had insisted on foreign touring with the Orchestra as a condition of signing on as Music Director. Since the fiasco with the State Department and Reiner in 1959, we had never received a single offer to tour outside of the United States and Canada until Solti arrived on the scene.

In the early autumn of 1971, Solti and the CSO were to take their first joint tour of Europe. It was scheduled for six weeks beginning with a week of recording for London Decca in Vienna, Austria. Carlo Maria Guilini was engaged as the Principal Guest Conductor for the tour to provide some occasional relief for Solti. Excitement in the Orchestra was extremely high. Everyone understood very well that if the forthcoming tour was successful, we could finally put the fiasco of 1959 behind us. Finally, the itinerary was finalized and travel plans were being made.

For one of the few times in his life, John Edwards made a mistake in judgment when he asked his assistant, Kenneth Meine, to arrange for the transportation. Anticipating that there may be some hitches when undertaking a totally new experience, the Members' Committee appointed a Tour Subcommittee to work with Meine on the travel plans. I was named as Chairman of that Tour Subcommittee.

Because he had shone so much interest in the workings of the Members' Committee, I asked Don Koss, the Timpanist, if he would work with me on this tour, and he agreed.

Within a relatively short time, Meine summoned us to his office to tell us that he had selected an air carrier that was willing to undertake the entire European tour for us. Its name was SpanTex, a supplemental air carrier based in Spain with U.S. offices in Texas. He told us that the only problem was that the carrier needed a firm commitment from us in just a few days.

The carrier's top executives arranged a hurried filmed presentation for us in the offices of The Orchestral Association. The presentation was very glitzy, emphasizing the quality of the service by attractive flight attendants and the gourmet quality of the on-board meal service. Koss and I were not impressed. We had heard nothing about the carrier's safety record or compliance with international standards of flight safety.

Fortunately, Meine was not authorized to go ahead unless he received our OK. Meine said the carrier needed an answer in just two days or the entire deal was off. We replied that if the answer was due that soon, it would have to be "No." We simply needed more time to come to a decision. Meine was absolutely beside himself.

Since we already had the complete itinerary for the tour, we asked for and received the total dollar figure for the air carrier's services. The price quoted us seemed exorbitant!

Within the next three days, Koss and I visited the local offices of three well-known major carriers, all of whom were members of IATA, the International Air Transport Association. We furnished each of them with our itinerary and asked for a total charter package price.

The lowest bid came from KLM, the Royal Dutch Airline. Their price was substantially less than that quoted us by SpanTex. We brought our figures and those we received from Meine to John Edwards. He was surprised and dismayed. While none of us actually verbalized it, there was a general understanding among us that Meine had tried to personally profit from the air transport provided by SpanTex, since the difference between its actual cost and the quoted cost could provide a nice kickback for Meine.

Since a contract was made with KLM to provide the Orchestra's transportation and the deal with SpanTex fell through, Meine had not committed a crime. However, Edwards quietly dismissed him the following year.

Since the orchestra and staff were to travel on the affinity charter provided by KLM, the spouses and family members accompanying the tour had to travel by alternative means. Rex Travel Organization, Inc. of Chicago was engaged to provide transportation for the family members that planned to go along on at least part of the tour. The President of Rex Travel asked me if I knew anyone willing to take the entire tour while acting as his representative en route. Without even asking her, I volunteered my wife, Charlotte, to act as the Family Members tour leader. The incentive, of course, was that Rex Travel would provide free transportation for her on the entire tour. It was the first and only benefit I ever received for representing the members of the Chicago Symphony.

Fortunately for me, my wife was more than willing to undertake the task of being Tour Leader for the family members. If she had not, I would have been in deep trouble.

So, as the summer turned into autumn in 1971, the Chicago Symphony Orchestra was poised to begin its first tour of Europe with Georg Solti and Carlo Maria Guilini as its conductors.

Chapter 13

Europe

The KLM Royal Dutch Airline gate at the International Terminal in Chicago's O'Hare Airport that September afternoon in 1971 was the gathering place for the musicians, stage hands and administrative staff, all of whom were about to embark on the CSO's first foreign tour. Passports were being checked and instrument cases small enough to accompany their owners were also having a final check. Nothing could afford to be left behind. We wouldn't be back here for another six weeks. Our wardrobe trunks and large instrument trunks, packed to the brim, were traveling to Vienna on another flight filled with nothing but cargo.

Family members traveling to Europe were on a later KLM line flight and were using this opportunity to see off their spouses before reuniting in Vienna. Charlotte had made up a large chart by which she kept track of the coming and going of everyone she was responsible for.

Our charter flight on KLM departed the gate right on time. The overnight flight was exceptionally smooth and the dinner served on board was excellent. I was glad that Koss and I had recommended KLM. If the arrangements for our transportation had been anything other than excellent, I fear we would never have heard the end of it from our colleagues.

Those who had hoped to get some sleep during the long trans-Atlantic flight were sadly disappointed. The problem traveling with so many people you know is that the conversations never end. A few of the musicians overindulged on the liquor being served and actually had to be helped off the plane when it arrived in Vienna early the next morning.

After clearing Austrian customs and immigration, we boarded waiting motor coaches for the drive to our various hotels. My wife and I were some of those staying at a hotel in Baden, a suburb of Vienna. It was a quaint town known for its thermal mineral baths. A walk down Baden's main street revealed a house at which composer Ludwig von Beethoven had lived for a time. Supposedly, Beethoven had composed his Pastoral Symphony there. The Orchestra had nothing scheduled that first day in Vienna and many of us used it to rest and recover from the jet lag.

The first service scheduled for us was the following morning. We rode motor coaches into the heart of Vienna. Just a few short blocks from the Ring Strasse that surrounds the center of the city, we were deposited at an old, nondescript, brown brick building known as the Sofiensaal. This was Decca's recording studio, the same one in which the Vienna Philharmonic Orchestra normally records. It certainly didn't look very impressive from the outside.

Actually, it was an old converted ballroom with a large wooden dance floor that was built over a bedrock thermal spring. Despite all the noises of the city's motor traffic that was going by out on the street, the interior of the Sofiensaal was deadly quiet and without vibrations of any kind. The ballroom had been one that was used for dancing during the heyday of Johann Strauss, Jr., the Viennese Waltz King.

The large rectangular wooden floor had temporary bleachers rising at both ends. The work we were to record was a massive symphony that employed a large orchestra, a huge mixed choir, a children's choir and eight vocal soloists. The work also called for an organ, a church bell and offstage brass band. All these forces were assembled to record Gustav Mahler's Symphony No. 8, known as *The Symphony of a Thousand*.

I found myself assigned to a spot at the top of the bleachers at the opposite end of the room from those used for the chorus. I was looking at Solti's back during the entire set of recording sessions, which I had never done before. There is a sensitive opening to the Symphony's Second Part, which required the recording engineers to isolate me in order to clearly, record some pianissimo cymbal notes I had to play.

Solti was a master at managing big productions like this with many participants. He enjoys being the Major Domo. The massive choir consisted of the members of the Vienna State Opera Choir, the Vienna Singverein and the Vienna Boys' Choir. He started the first session by lecturing the choir in German. He told them that they were now going to sing with an orchestra that did not make mistakes. He asked them to be very careful and mistake free when they sang. After tuning very carefully, we started with the First Part of the Symphony.

Over the course of the years, I have played in many different settings, some of whose acoustics were horrible and others only less so. I don't think that any of us were prepared for the absolutely incredible acoustics of the Sofiensaal. We produced the richest orchestral sound there that I have ever heard. Some of the family members who were there on the sidelines as guests were moved to uncontrollable tears. The Sofiensaal surpassed even the fabulous acoustics of New York's Carnegie Hall.

The shame of the entire project was that this massive collection of singers and instrumentalists never performed together in a concert hall before a live audience. The entire performance was for the benefit of a recording, and nothing more. But, in all candor, the experience of doing this recording in Vienna at the Sofiensaal was the musical highlight of my professional career. It was somewhat like an epiphany for me, the closest experience I had had to a religious one. The memory of it will stay with me the rest of my days. I still cannot listen to our recording of Mahler's Symphony No. 8 made in Vienna without being profoundly moved.

The intense recording sessions lasted the better part of a week. Just outside the ballroom in the outer corridor, there was a small buffet counter staffed by amiable Viennese women. The hot dogs we Americans love so much, and which are sometimes called "Wieners", originated in Vienna. In fact, "Wieners" means "of Vienna" and the buffet at the Sofiensaal served up some of the best I have ever tasted.

Rather than being served on a bun as they are in the U.S., they are served plain, in pairs, with a slice or two of delicious rye bread. If you also want mustard, you have to ask for it. When doing so, you must never, I mean never, omit the word, "bitte", German for "please." So if you needed some delicious nourishment during one of the breaks in the recording session, you would hurry to the little buffet counter and ask for, "Ein paar wurstel, bitte, mit senf." They are served on a paper plate with a plastic fork and knife. If you wanted a small bottle of orange soda to wash your meal down, you had to ask for "ein orangen bombe, bitte."

After the recordings ended, we played a single concert at the Vienna Grosser Musicvereinsaal, the wonderful concert hall that the televised New Year's Day concerts have made familiar to many Americans. Boston's Symphony Hall was designed with the Musicvereinsaal as a model. Once we left Vienna, the real touring began.

We flew all the way to Glasgow, Scotland, where the last Jewish Bagpipe Band in Scotland met us on the tarmac, in uniform. It was there to greet a native son, David Greenbaum, one of our 'Cellists, who was born in Glasgow and still had a Scotch brogue thick enough to be cut by a knife. Greenbaum descended the stairway from the plane with his traditional tam on, and was in all his glory. His brother still lived there and arranged for the bagpipe band greeting.

Glasgow, however, was not our destination. That city appeared too poverty stricken to afford a concert by the CSO. We were met at the airport by motor coaches that carried us Northward to Edinburgh, where we performed at Usher Hall. Strangely, that hall had no dressing facilities. So we were obligated to change into our formal clothes in full view of the early arrivals at the hall. It was experiences like that taught us that modesty is a luxury that is not always available on tour.

We worked our way South through London, Paris and Brussels, etc. Our receptions everywhere were absolutely phenomenal. Very often, the applause at the end of a concert lasted so long and through so many curtain calls, that Solti would have to lead the musicians off the stage.

We had an interesting experience in Belgium, where in addition to concerts in Brussels, we also played a concert in Ghent. The hall in Ghent was a very old facility that truly had no dressing space whatsoever. Our entourage of motor coaches had to slowly wind its way through the narrow streets of Ghent to an old, dirty warehouse. There, our wardrobe trunks had been set up and we filed in and changed into our formal attire amid many calls of "Baa, baa, baa." If we had to behave like sheep, we may as well sound like sheep.

Then, in our formal clothes, our coaches wound their way back through the same narrow streets to take us to the concert hall. The city residents who had seen us on the way to the warehouse probably thought we were simply a group of tourists. But when they saw us again some thirty minutes later all dressed up in our formal white tie and tails, I'm sure they didn't know what to make of it all!

We continued through the heart of Europe, even flying into West Berlin's Templehof Airport on an Air France jet. Only the aircraft of the occupying powers, Britain, France and the U.S. were authorized to fly over East German territory on their way into West Berlin in those days. We performed a marvelous concert in the modern Berlin Philharmonie, home of the Berlin Philharmonic.

While in Berlin, we stayed at the Kempinski Hotel just off the Kurfurstendamm, West Berlin's principal shopping street. Across the street from our hotel was the modern Judische Gemeindhaus, the Jewish Community Center, whose façade had been the front of Berlin's largest synagogue before it was burned to the ground on Krystal Nacht. Inside, there were many photographs of pre-World War II Jewish life in Berlin. Some of the CSO's Jewish members who toured the Center left in tears.

The tour continued on with Guilini conducting occasional concerts in the less prestigious centers. Solti was in charge of every concert that really mattered. By the end of the tour, Guilini was not very pleased with the concerts he had been assigned to conduct by Solti.

I recall that my wife and I ran into him and his family just as they left the Notre Dame cathedral in Paris on a Sunday morning. We stopped to chat for a few moments. He was always very cordial to members of the CSO whom he knew. He spoke of his role on the tour as being "somewhat disappointing", but he was never one to whine and complain. He was too much of a gentleman to do that.

The tour finally wound up in London where we performed in the Royal Festival Hall on the banks of the Thames. The Orchestra was exhausted, but exhilarated beyond words. The tour had been an outstanding artistic success. The Chicago Symphony Orchestra was now being spoken about in the same breath with the Berlin and Vienna Philharmonics and the other great orchestras of the world. It had taken us twelve years to recoup from the Reiner debacle of 1959. It never would have happened without the engagement of Georg Solti as the Music Director of the Chicago Symphony Orchestra. We weren't doing at all badly, especially considering that our Music Director was a third choice selection!

The next year, the recording we made in Vienna's Sofiensaal earned a record three Grammys: Album of the Year, Best Classical Performance—Choral, and Best Engineered Recording—Classical. If you listen carefully to this recording, you will recognize that the quality of the sound is unlike any recording made by London Records in Chicago. We can thank the Sofiensaal for that!

Chapter 14

A New Era Begins

Our arrival back in Chicago was as festive as any occasion I can remember. We were treated like returning conquering heroes. If we had been the Chicago Bears football team, just returning from winning the Super Bowl, the adulation could not have been greater.

The entire Orchestra was seated on special floats on which we rode in a ticker tape parade down La Salle Street, the city's financial district. The crowds along the curbs were three and four deep, all yelling and cheering. The parade was followed by a reception in the Council Chambers of City Hall. There, Mayor Richard J. Daley lauded the Orchestra for having shone the cities of Europe that Chicago had more to offer culturally than the memories of Al Capone. Solti was presented with an enormous trophy from the Mayor, which he graciously accepted on behalf of the Orchestra. Every individual member of the Chicago Symphony was presented with a signed "Certificate of Merit" from the Mayor and City Council of Chicago.

Both houses of the Illinois Legislature passed resolutions honoring the Chicago Symphony Orchestra and the Chicago Press Club designated us as "Chicagoans of the Year." The members of the Percussion section additionally received individual Plaques of Appreciation from William F. and Maggie Ludwig, the owners of the Ludwig Drum Company, the world's best known manufacturer of percussion instruments, then manufactured in Chicago.

Marquis, producers of *Who's Who In America*, requested copies of our biographical sketches for inclusion in their reference work. The honors we received were unbelievable. These were not the kinds of things that normally happened to members of an American symphony orchestra. It was almost impossible to remember that we had been a downtrodden group of musicians who were merely trying their best to eke out a living, never dreaming that one day, we would be treated like rock superstars.

The 1971 tour of Europe changed the perceptions we had of ourselves forever. We were no longer anonymous. We were individuals of value who now had greater expectations from our professional lives. We now viewed the world through eyes that had a different perspective. We now know that musicians can make important contribution to the quality of life of those who love classical music. How one feels about themselves is vitally important to every individual. And the way we felt about ourselves was simply grand.

The 1971 tour of Europe was the beginning of a different life for the members of the Chicago Symphony. The lives of those who participated in that tour were changed forever. We were no longer a group of nobodies who could be easily manipulated by others for their own purposes. In effect, that was the gift that Georg Solti bestowed on the musicians of the CSO.

Our perspective on the negotiations for new contracts had us asking for improvements that we never would have dreamed of previously. I now had my own personal agenda of conditions that I wanted improved. These were intended to value the personal contribution that every member of the Orchestra made to the whole.

For many years, String players were frozen into a hierarchy of positions within a section. Being permanently assigned to the third stand, inside, of the First Violins, for instance, placed one in a superior position to one assigned to the fifth stand, outside. The closer the assigned position was to the front of the Orchestra or the conductor, the higher you were in the pecking order.

This artificial valuation of the worth of each player in their section had long been the norm in every orchestra. What this did was to devalue every player who was not in a position at the front of the orchestra. It also created a self-defeating competition for a seat at the front of your section.

This artificial hierarchy also meant that you were always seated next to the same stand partner, perhaps for many years. This created a stagnant situation that deprived each musician of any incentive for improvement.

I suggested that the members of the String sections should revolve within their section, changing partners every two weeks. For instance, each outside player would advance one stand every two weeks while the inside players moved back one stand. When one reached the front of their section, they would move laterally and then begin moving backward.

The string players I spoke to were very enthusiastic about the idea of revolving positions and would visualize all sorts of benefits such rotation would provide. They especially liked the idea of playing with a different partner every two weeks and the challenges that would provide.

This system of rotation could work in an orchestra like the Chicago Symphony in which each string player is actually a very talented and capable musician.

The idea became popular among the string players, and the idea became a proposal for a subsequent contract negotiation. It was finally adopted within a system where the first two stands in each of the First and Second Violins remained fixed while the balance of the sections revolved.

In the Viola, 'Cello and Bass sections, only the first stand remained fixed. Actually, that made sense because these fixed stands contained the players that were the Principals and Assistant Principals of their respective sections. In effect, the String sections came out of a feudal concept into a democratic one.

81

During our first foreign tour, the Music Director, Manager and other supervisory personnel rode in the First Class section of the plane while all the musicians were seated in Coach. Initially, that was not a problem because on a charter, there was enough seats in Coach to allow an empty seat between virtually every musician.

Eventually, the rules on charter flights changed and we were forced to purchase block of tickets on regular line flights. Gone was the luxury of empty seats to relieve the congestion.

That was when I suggested that everyone in the entire company, other than the Music Director, ought to rotate into whatever empty seats there were in first class. There was no valid reason for a manager to always ride in First Class while every musician rode in Coach. Certainly, records would have to be maintained, but that was a small price to pay for making each musician feel like he or she was an important part of this company.

This subject reminds me of a tale we heard about the way Fritz Reiner and his wife rode in planes. Years after Reiner had passed on, one of our Clarinet players, Walter Wollwage, was booking a Swiss Air flight to Europe for a vacation. During the course of his conversation with the ticket agent, Wollwage happened to mention that he was a member of the Chicago Symphony Orchestra.

"Oh," the agent said. "Did you know that whenever Fritz Reiner and his wife would travel to Europe from Chicago, they would always travel via Swiss Air?" the agent asked.

"No," replied our Clarinet player, "I didn't know that."

"As a matter of fact, I always booked their flights," said the ticket agent with some pride. "Did you know that whenever they traveled to Europe, he rode in First Class while she rode in Coach?" The agent and Wollwage had a good laugh together.

A few years later, the CSO happened to be in New York for a series of concerts at Carnegie Hall. The dates happened to coincide with the tenth anniversary of Reiner's death. Robert Sherman, of Radio Station WQXR, used the occasion to present a retrospective on Reiner's life on his program, "Listening Booth." He invited a number of the CSO's Principal players and me (I don't know why I was invited other than the fact that I was known to be a fair storyteller) who had worked with Reiner to have a discussion about his life and his music making. Also invited to participate was Carlotta Reiner, the late conductor's widow. She had come down to New York from her Westport, Connecticut home for the occasion.

It was hardly a somber occasion. Mrs. Reiner, who had been a single actress back in the late 1920's while Reiner was the Music Director of the Cincinnati Symphony, had been caught with Reiner in a hotel room there while the Maestro was still married to a previous wife. The scandal eventually led to his dismissal from that orchestra.

As we filed into the radio studio, Mrs. Reiner greeted every one of us by our first names. She was absolutely delighted to be with all of us again. She was dressed in a pleated wool plaid skirt with a numbered football jersey for a top.

The next two hours were filled with funny personal recollections of experiences with Reiner. Mrs. Reiner joined in the fun and told a few new stories we had never heard before. She recalled one occasion when they were in Europe together and paid a visit to Richard Strauss, the composer with whom Reiner had often collaborated while he was the conductor of the Dresden Opera as a young man.

When Reiner introduced her, he told Strauss in German, "Das is meine jetstege Frau," which translated into "This is my current wife." Actually, I believe that Carlotta was his third wife.

She was so thrilled to meet Strauss that she told him how much she enjoyed a certain aria he had written in his opera, *Electra*, and started to sing the aria in her untrained voice. After just a few moments, Reiner told his wife, "All right, all right, that's enough of that!"

The radio program, in which we all participated, went on for two hours. It was interspersed with recordings we had made with Reiner. All of us enjoyed the encounter immensely. Of course, we could all speak freely now. Even Mrs. Reiner sensed that. It was the last time that any of us ever saw her.

Chapter 15

Ouch

It was during the middle 1970's that I began having health problems. After seeing many physicians, I learned that I had chronic kidney stone disease. I was experiencing frequent abdominal pains that the doctors believed were not being caused by my single kidney stone. They believed I had developed a spastic colon or chronic colitis, and attributed my abdominal pains to that condition. They turned out to be wrong, as we shall see.

Nevertheless, I continued working as best I could, suffering in silence on many occasions. Dealing with the intermittent pain and the subsequent medications I had been prescribed to take did take their toll. I had far less energy than I had been used to having and this made me curtail many of the activities that I would normally be doing.

I gave up my chairmanship of the Members' Committee, which was now occupied by Koss. His work with me when we were able to obtain the services of KLM for our tour of Europe in '71 put him in good stead with the other Committee members. Because he still had much to learn at the time, he would often phone me at home several times a day and ask questions. My wife used to say he was "picking my brains."

In time, he was able to provide excellent leadership for the Members' Committee. As mentioned previously, he had this uncanny ability to remember everything he heard and saw.

At the times we would be negotiating new contracts, usually every three years, he provided very skillful leadership for our negotiating team and many gains were made in our working conditions and wages.

We were finally able to convert the gratuitous pension The Orchestral Association had been providing for the Orchestra's musicians into an independent pension trust. William Scarlett, a member of the Orchestra's Trumpet section, and I were appointed the plan's Trustees representing the Orchestra's musicians, while Chaukley J. Hambleton, retired President of the Harris Bank, and William Searle, an officer of the G.D. Searle Company, developers of *Aspartame*, the artificial sweetener used in *Nutrasweet* and *Equal*, were the Trustees representing The Orchestral Association. I was able to serve as a Trustee of the Pension Plan for nine years, many of them as Chairman of the Trust.

Working on the Pension Trust with these very knowledgeable businessmen was a wonderful experience and taught me much about financial matters and managing a multimillion-dollar enterprise. There were just so many opportunities that were opened up to me as a result of being placed in a position of leadership in this world-class cultural institution.

All of this time, Michael Greenfield, one of the union's attorneys that had been installed by the AFM Trustee, Hal C. Davis, assisted the Members' Committee, the Pension Trust and the union's negotiating team. We did most of the bargaining with the management team while Greenfield would put our agreements into legally binding language.

Even Dan Garamoni, President of Local 10-208, turned out to be a supportive, if not skilful, leader. Who knows, perhaps Jimmy Petrillo was pretty clever after all when he chose Garamoni as his "heir apparent." Of course, it should be remembered that Garamoni might never have been President of the union had it not been for the crooked machinations of Leo Nye, the union's Recording Secretary, and others who had managed to manipulate the election of Garamoni and Nye in 1962 at the behest of "the boys."

That was all water under the bridge now as we settled into a more stable relationship within the Orchestra with management. Gone was the intrigue of earlier days, the worries of dealing with a miserable conductor and the concerns of earning a year-round livelihood. Solti was always a pleasure to deal with.

The Chicago Symphony Orchestra was riding high. Solti, who had now been knighted by Queen Elizabeth II, was featured on the cover of *Time* magazine, and described as *The Fastest Baton in the West*. We were doing plenty of recording, winter and summer. At Ravinia, we had the good fortune of having the talented Seiji Ozawa and James Levine as successive Music Directors. Each of these leaders had done an inordinate amount of recording with us during their summer residencies.

Some of our recordings were also being used in the sound tracks of Hollywood motion pictures. *Catch 22* with Alan Arkin, and *Dead Poets Society* with Robin Williams, each used our recordings on their sound tracks. Of course, whenever that would happen, we would be paid an additional fee.

We began traveling abroad every few years, primarily to the major cities of Europe. In 1977, however, we made an historic three-week tour of Japan, which was phenomenally successful. The Japanese tour was one of the most enjoyable tours the Orchestra has ever taken. We traveled the length and breath of Japan and performed in some of the best new concert halls we had ever had the pleasure of working in. All of our concerts were sold out with one notable exception.

In Hiroshima, we had only a three-quarters filled hall. Perhaps the inhabitants of that unlucky city may have forgiven us for our use of the atomic bomb, but they still haven't forgotten what we did there.

It is a painful reminder of the excesses of war to visit the Peace Memorial Park in Hiroshima. It was constructed around the epicenter of the area in which the bomb was dropped. To go through the Peace Museum that is adjacent to the park is extremely painful and reminiscent of Yad Vashem, the memorial to the victims of the Holocaust in Jerusalem, Israel.

The Japanese tour was the last tour for James Lane, the newest member of our Percussion section. The year before the Japanese tour, he had undergone surgery for a malignant brain tumor. For a time, he was doing well after his surgery. He was able to go on the tour with his wife and elder daughter. We had many memorable times together in the course of the Japanese tour, times that I will be recalling for the rest of my life. The year after the tour, however, his malignancy became active again and he slowly died. He left behind a young wife and two young daughters. He had been a member of the Chicago Symphony Orchestra for only eleven years and was replaced by James Ross, son of James J. Ross in 1979.

James Ross, the younger, was the winner of an audition process that included over a hundred applicants from all over the country. I was delighted that he joined the Orchestra because I had known him since he was a toddler in Pittsburgh.

With all the success the Chicago Symphony was enjoying, I nevertheless had a feeling that everything was not as it should be. Perhaps things were too good! It was extremely difficult to put my finger on it, and sometimes, I thought I was being unduly paranoiac about my feelings. Perhaps, I thought, I had been jaded by all my experiences and was feeling something that simply did not exist. On the surface, everything was very good in the Orchestra, but I kept having these nagging feelings that I just could not dismiss.

Then, several things happened that I never believed would happen. Perhaps, these things go on to some degree in many large and successful institutions. But I had never been aware of what I was about to experience, and I didn't know what, if anything, I could do about them. Telling others what I had learned would have been useless because they would not have believed what I was prepared to tell them. It was an extremely frustrating position that I was in because what I learned was about activities that I would never be able to prove. Perhaps, they existed only in my tortured mind. Or perhaps, carrying out these corrupt acts had become so sophisticated that these activities were somehow shielded. I will let you be the judge.

The activities I am about to describe have been going on for many years and are now probably so institutionalized that little can be done to stop them. A smattering of knowledge can be a very dangerous thing.

In the early 1970's, I decided that with all the legal matters I was now dealing with, it would be very beneficial to have a formal legal education. The problem was that my formal education ended when I graduated high school in

1941. In order to enter law school, I would need an undergraduate degree from a university.

I investigated my local options and decided to enroll in a special degree program being offered by Roosevelt University, only a few blocks away from Orchestra Hall, down Michigan Avenue. I could attend classes there while working with the Symphony. So, thirty years after I graduated high school, I started working on my bachelor's degree.

Through attending classes, taking equivalency tests and receiving credit for life experiences, I completed enough credits to earn a degree in General Studies, with an emphasis on Labor Education, in two and a half years. It was quite an experience to receive my baccalaureate degree in the old Auditorium Theater, the site of the CSO's first concerts in 1891.

My acceptance by, and enrollment in, the John Marshall Law School followed that. One of the Symphony's Bassoonists, Burl Lane, started law school there at the same time as I did, and we attended many classes together. It was an intellectual pursuit that I enjoyed immensely, despite all the work it involved. But sad to say, especially for a Percussionist, my timing was not good.

After successfully completing the first semester of law school, the Orchestra's increased touring activity made it impossible to continue. At John Marshall, if one missed two class sessions, one could not even sit for the final exam in that subject. There was no way I could now juggle working with the Symphony and attending law school at the same time. Regrettably, neither Lane nor I were able to complete our studies.

In the course of meeting with Michael Greenfield, the union's attorney, I would often travel to his La Salle Street law offices. There, I would usually have to wait for a time until he finished working on whatever he was doing. It would usually not be very long before he would invite me into his office after which we would sit and chat about whatever I had come to see him about.

On one such occasion, I happened to come over to the Asher, Greenfield & Gubbins offices while they were being completely redecorated. Even the firm's reception area was in a mess. I was patiently waiting in an area just outside Greenfield's office where there were many desks, and files were stacked everywhere in their client folders.

Having nothing better to do at the moment, I happened to glance down at the stack of folders that were sitting on a nearby desk. What I saw startled me because the client's name on the top folder was "The Orchestral Association." Just beneath the name of the client was a line for the subject matter, which turned out to be a very innocuous and mundane question.

At first, the significance of what I had seen didn't have much meaning to me. But then, I stopped to think about what I had seen. Now The Orchestral Association employs it own law firm, Mayer, Brown & Platt. It is one of the largest and most prestigious in all of Chicago. I thought, *Why would The Orchestral Association be utilizing the firm of Asher, Greenfield & Gubbins, the union's attorneys, for any legal work whatsoever when they have their own competent legal counsel?*

There was no easy answer to my question. Was this simply a legitimate quest for legal information that their own learned legal counsel could not supply? That seemed highly unlikely. The law firm of Mayer, Brown & Platt occupies several of the upper floors of the Sears Tower and employs a virtual army of attorneys and paralegals.

What made my question so important is that labor and management, as those terms are known in labor relations, are supposed to be in a relationship that is at arm's length and adversarial. Under such constraints, one party should not be dealing with the other in a manner that could jeopardize their independent status.

What appeared to be happening here was that the employer was apparently paying the union's attorneys for services that could be interpreted as a conflict of interest. The interesting part is that attorneys for both sides are required to avoid even the appearance of a conflict of interest. That was totally absent here.

What made matters worse was the fact such payments could easily be hidden in The Orchestral Association's books as merely a legal expense. Furthermore, communications between any lawyer and his client are privileged. Neither lawyer nor client can be compelled to reveal the true nature of their relationship.

Of course, I never asked anyone at either the union's law firm or The Orchestral Association what this legal work was all about. To have done so may have placed my career, and perhaps even my life, in jeopardy! So, to this day, I have no definitive answer to my question. But my new knowledge certainly changed how I dealt with both management and the union from that day on. I have answered my own question to my own satisfaction. What conclusion others may arrive at regarding the above is their own business.

Chapter 16

New Perspective

Once I made the discoveries I had stumbled onto that fateful day outside Michael Greenfield's office, I became very circumspect in my relations with virtually everyone. It was like a curse had been placed on me. I tried an experiment.

Generally, when there was a meeting of the Trustees of the Chicago Symphony Orchestra Pension Trust, they would take place in a conference room at either the Harris Bank or at the offices of one of the fund's advisors. Michael Greenfield, the union's attorney, and Stuart Bernstein, the Association's attorney on labor relations matters, would attend all of these meetings. These meetings were usually scheduled to coincide with the end of a CSO rehearsal. William Scarlett and I would very often walk over to the meeting's site together.

I told Scarlett on this particular occasion only that I thought I could now predict with some degree of certainty how Greenfield would react to any question put to him in the course of the meeting. I did not reveal how, or upon what basis, I would attempt to make such predictions. He was a little surprised at what I had offered, but not unduly alarmed. Perhaps he thought I was just trying to impress him.

In any case, during the course of the meeting, questions would arise in which we requested the opinions of our respective attorneys. When such a question would arise and Greenfield might spend a few moments considering his answer, I would simply whisper in Scarlett's ear what I thought Greenfield's response might be. More often than not, my predictions proved to be correct. When the meeting was over and Scarlett and I would usually head in different directions for the trip home, he asked how I was able to make the predictions I did. Of course, I couldn't reveal my secret.

All I had done was put myself in Greenfield's place and figure what the answer would be in order to favor The Orchestral Association's interests. I was usually correct. This little experiment confirmed, at least in my own mind, what the true relationship between the employer and the union was.

When I thought back to the days of the AFM's imposition of a trusteeship on the union and the AFM's replacement of Francis Heisler and Marc Schwartz with the firm of Asher, Greenfield & Gubbins, I remembered something else that happened then.

At one of our regular Saturday evening series concerts at Orchestra Hall, I happened to notice that the center box, one of the most valued locations in Orchestra Hall from the standpoint of prestige, was now occupied by none other than Les Asher, his wife and their friends. Les Asher was the founder and senior partner of Asher, Greenfield & Gubbins. Prior to that surprise appearance, I had not even known that he was a music lover or had ever attended a concert of the Chicago Symphony. Now, he regularly occupied the center box.

To understand the significance of this appearance, these prestigious boxes are generally owned by very wealthy families and handed down to their heirs. There were families in Chicago that would almost kill to gain possession of one of these center boxes. Yet, suddenly, after Asher's law firm becomes the musicians' union attorneys, he is somehow put in possession of this important location.

I didn't attach any particular significance to this event at the time. At a minimum, I thought merely that the Association was extending some good will and was trying to butter up the union's attorney. Now, I viewed it as part of a grand scheme to compromise the union.

When I started to look around, more evidence appeared to reveal itself to me, affirming that my conclusions were probably correct. This time, it was very close to home. Although I was no longer Chairman of the CSO Members' Committee, I continued to serve on the bargaining team at the negotiations of new contracts for the Orchestra.

As the negotiations were concluding for a new contract during the middle 1970's, and we were finally down to the point where new provisions or dollar amounts were finally being decided, Don Koss, the Committee's new Chairman, started to predict what the final outcome would be. He would whisper them into my ear because I was usually seated right next to him. I couldn't imagine how he could be so clairvoyant. Every one of his predictions was right on the money.

When I thought about it later, I asked myself how he could have been so accurate in his predictions. It was then that I suddenly realized that he could only have known if he had been in on an earlier secret meeting at which these matters were decided. Were the negotiations going on at two different levels? Were these decisions being made in secret by just a few people on each side of the bargaining table? Were the sessions that others and I were attending merely a charade?

These questions were spinning around in my head. Had Koss been compromised somehow? If he was, what had been the consideration he received and how could the management conceal such payments? I realized then that having relinquished my leadership of the Committee might have resulted in some dire consequences for the members of the Orchestra. I had the feeling that I had been placed in a box with a gag over my mouth. Now I finally knew what had been nagging me for so long.

Apparently, things were not as they had seemed. Conditions in the Orchestra were good, but apparently manipulated. Was this a symphonic paradox? There was no way of knowing where we would be if the integrity of the Orchestra's representatives were not being compromised as I concluded. Perhaps, it was market forces after all, and not the militancy of the Orchestra's members, that was driving the quality of our pay and working conditions. After all, many of the nation's orchestras were now staffed with really excellent musicians, and the competition for the services of the best was fierce.

Rather than resolve any feelings I may have had about the Orchestra, I was now in the dilemma of not being able to do anything about what I believed were the missteps of those involved. I decided to make plans for my own retirement from the Chicago Symphony Orchestra. I no longer wanted to be involved in a situation which had spun out of control and over which I had absolutely no control.

From the very beginning, I knew that if I became a permanent member of the Chicago Symphony Orchestra, my employment was not guaranteed for life. I would never own my job. It was only temporary at best. I believed that thirty years would be all that I was entitled to if I was lucky enough to make this my career.

By 1984, I believed that I had fulfilled my time in this great orchestra. I simply knew too much and had experienced too much for my own good. I suspected that others had an inkling of what I knew. As it was, my health was not improving and maintaining my competence was becoming more and more challenging as time went on.

Then, a medical miracle took place! I read somewhere that a German company had invented a machine called a Shock Wave Lithotripter. This machine used sound shock waves to disintegrate kidney stones into very fine particles, which could then be passed spontaneously.

During the course of my illness, I had even gone to the Mayo Clinic in Rochester, Minnesota for help. They believed that the cause of my abdominal pains was the result of my now mothball sized kidney stone, and not from a spastic colon. They suggested surgery to remove the kidney stone, but I hesitated because of the risks involved. I had a horseshoe, or fused kidney. In such cases, physicians could not be sure exactly where the kidneys' blood vessels were routed. The surgery seemed too risky to me and I declined their recommendation.

But now, there was the German Lithotripter. I made an appointment with my urologist to ask whether in his opinion, I would make a good candidate for a lithotripsy. He agreed that I would be, but at the time, it was still experimental and there were only five such machines in the entire United States.

Somehow, he managed to get me on the list for the procedure at the Methodist Hospital in Indianapolis, Indiana. There were no such machines in Chicago at the time. The problem was whether my health insurance would cover the cost of the procedure. After a good bit of negotiations, the insurance carrier finally agreed to pay for the procedure.

On an August day in 1984, after the Ravinia season had concluded, my wife and I drove to Indianapolis where I checked into Methodist Hospital. It took two treatments by the Lithotripter to completely break down my kidney stone. By the time I was coming out of the anesthesia, I was already starting to feel better. The procedure was, as they say, "A piece of cake." The following day, my wife and I drove back to Chicago. From that time to this, I have never had any of the symptoms I suffered with for the previous dozen years. I was completely pain free!

I was now prepared to retire that October when a glitch arose. It would be the final battle of my career in the CSO.

Chapter 17

Finale

There was one last impediment that stood in the way of my retirement. I was in my early 60's now and would not be covered by Medicare until I reached 65. The contract between the union and management had a provision that provided healthcare coverage for those retiring before age 65. However, there was a proviso that predicated the continuation of healthcare on whether the insurance carrier granted coverage. Since I had been hospitalized many times during the dozen years I suffered with my kidney stone, the insurance carrier denied me coverage.

Of course, I appealed the denial of coverage. I argued that the proviso, which granted the carrier the discretion to provide coverage, was discriminatory. If the coverage was provided for early retirees only when the insurance carrier deemed to extend it, then the proviso could be used to grant coverage to some and deny it to others on a totally capricious basis. That made the coverage discriminatory on its face, particularly when the criteria the carrier would use to make its decisions were a complete mystery.

The battle raged on for the better part of a year. Had I not protested the medical coverage proviso while still an employee, I would have lost the right to do so once the employment relationship was severed. So I had no choice. I could not afford to retire until I knew I had healthcare coverage.

By the end of my thirty-first year, I was informed that the insurance company had relented. From that time on, coverage would be extended to all early retirees regardless of the condition of their health. I had won my last battle for justice and was prepared to retire.

I informed management that I would retire on October 5, 1985, the anniversary of my engagement as a Percussionist. That was a Saturday, and the Orchestra had a concert scheduled for that evening. The program included the Tschaikovsky 1812 Overture, the same composition that got my friend, Harry Brabec, into trouble with Fritz Reiner so many years ago. Of course, we no longer used shotguns to simulate the cannon shots. Merely touching a pad that triggered an electronically simulated cannon shot on a synthesizer fired the "shots".

I was informed that the Orchestra's new Manager, Henry Fogel, would make a presentation to me at the conclusion of the intermission after the entire Orchestra was reassembled on stage. The only composition I would perform that evening was the 1812 Overture's Cannon part. So I wasn't required to dress in formal clothing because I would be working back-stage with the help of audio and video monitors.

When the time came for the presentation, with the Orchestra assembled on stage and Sir Georg Solti on the podium, Henry Fogel and I came to center stage in front of the conductor's podium. Fogel made a speech to the audience about my retirement being a "rite of passage." I was then presented with the Theodore Thomas Medallion, for distinguished service to The Chicago Symphony Orchestra 1954—1985. Henry Fogel draped the medallion's ribbon about my neck and I stepped up to the microphone to say a few words.

My remarks included the following passage: "I am especially grateful for the opportunity to have worked with some of the finest musicians in the world for so many years, and you're looking at them right here on this stage." That line brought down the house. Even Sir Georg patted me on the back. And suddenly, my days with the Chicago Symphony were over.

The following month, my wife and I moved to San Diego, California, where we resided the next seven years. While there, I worked as an extra Percussionist with the San Diego Symphony and with the Seattle Symphony while they were on tour in Southern California. I also worked as a self-employed labor relations consultant. My first clients were the musicians of the Seattle Symphony Orchestra.

Randy Baunton, the Seattle orchestra's Principal Percussionist and Chairman of its committee contacted me to assist their players' organization in setting up a new and independent labor organization. They had become disenchanted with the Seattle AFM Local and sought to decertify it. This undertaking was successful in winning the representation rights for the musicians of the Seattle Symphony, the Seattle Opera, and the NW Ballet Orchestra. Their organization is called the International Guild of Symphony, Opera and Ballet Musicians and they maintain a website at www.igsobm.org.

But the activity that really got me into trouble all over again, notwithstanding the above, was the representation of a pair of married musicians who were members of the Los Angeles Philharmonic Orchestra. For having complained to their management of their harassment by the daughter of the Orchestra's Personnel Manager, they were brought up on charges before Local 47, AFM by the Personnel Manager.

Upon my advice, they resigned from the union and refused to stand trial for having exercised their civil rights. The union tried them *in absentia* and fined them each $500. Upon my advice, the fines were never paid. However, the Orchestra management continued to check-off their union dues without their permission.

Unfair labor practice charges were filed against Los Angeles AFM Local 47 in accordance with the U.S. Supreme Court's decision in *Communications*

Workers of America v. Beck. After some four years in which that case was pending, we won a settlement from the union which required them to return all the dues plus interest that had been illegally collected since these two musicians resigned from the union. It may have been the very first decision under the court's ruling in *Beck*. That was a very embarrassing result for both the union and the L.A. Philharmonic because they were required to post NLRB notices in the workplace and at the union hall that the parties would no longer engage in such activities.

From that time on, both the AFM and every American symphony orchestra in the nation having contracts with the AFM have apparently placed me on a Black List. I have not been engaged to perform a single professional engagement since.

And it all started because I didn't believe the members of the Chicago Symphony Orchestra owed Fritz Reiner an apology. That is truly the symphonic paradox, because no one watching and listening to one of our great American orchestras would ever believe that the artists that make up these ensembles could be treated so cavalierly by their employers and those who purport to represent them. These employers and unions are not-for-profit institutions that are subsidized by American taxpayers in the form of tax-free income.

Because some of what I accomplished during my years in the CSO, I was able to improve the profession of symphony musicians in ways that were both large and small. I have no apologies to offer anyone for what I did. If I had my life to live over again, I would probably live it in exactly the same way as I did.

So, the next time you attend a live symphony orchestra concert, I hope that you will consider for a moment that the musicians on stage are not anonymous, they are flesh and blood individuals who have the same aspirations as all of us who toil to earn a living for ourselves and our families. Also remember that things may not be what they seem. That is the nature of life in the United States, where outrage is something of the past. Justice can only come to those who pursue it because they believe in it.

Sam Denov

About the Author

A native Chicagoan, Sam Denov is a musician recognized throughout the world as one of America's best known symphonic percussionists. He has been honored many times and his biographical sketch has been featured in *Who's Who In America* and *Who's Who In Entertainment* for three decades. Following service in the U.S. Navy during WWII, he was a member of the San Antonio and Pittsburgh Symphony Orchestras, and most notably, the Chicago Symphony Orchestra for thirty-one years.

He has been featured in educational film and on video, most recently on the video series, *Concert Percussion, A Performer's Guide*, distributed by Warner Bros. Publications. He is also the author of many articles in trade publications and an educational text, *The Art of Playing the Cymbals*, also distributed by Warner Bros.

Denov has been heard on countless recordings, in concert throughout Europe, the Orient and South America, and on television and radio. He now performs, writes and lectures throughout the United States. He and his wife, Charlotte, reside in a suburb of Chicago.

Printed in the United States
92167LV00008B/92/A

9 780759 675438